Epic Journey from Mediocrity to Greatness

Unearthing your Unique Calling and Fulfilling your Earthly Purpose

(by the author of Hydrate to Elevate)

Dr. Debi Prasad Acharjya

Responsibility and Results Disclaimer

Welcome to your personal transformation guide. I am here to share insights that have spurred growth and radical transformation for many, including myself. However, I must clarify that I offer guidance, not guarantees. The journey you are about to embark on is yours alone, and the outcomes depend entirely on your efforts.

The essence of *Epic Journey from Mediocrity to Greatness* is that it is your unique journey to take, and the results you achieve are solely in your hands. Please keep in mind that the ideas presented in the book are based on my personal experience and should not be taken as professional advice. I encourage you to seek professional help whenever needed, step forward with courage, and embrace the adventure that lies ahead!

As your guide and fellow traveller on this path of personal transformation, I am here to share valuable insights that have helped both myself and countless others achieve radical transformation and growth. But let me clarify one thing: I am not here to make promises or save anyone.

I invite you to take the first step on your path of personal transformation, and I wish you all the courage, resilience, and joy on the adventure ahead.

Special Image Disclaimer

Images depicted are AI-generated and from "Shutterstock" images labelled as "Editorial use only." (Generally defined as use made for descriptive or illustrative purposes in a newsworthy context or of human interest. One of the common ways to permissibly use editorial content include "nonfiction books."

Contents

Foreword

His Excellency Prof. Dr. Sir Lakshman Madurasinghe
Chairman - Medicina Alternativa Alma Ata 1962
Senior Professor - Azteca University North America
Grand Chancellor - E.M.H Order knights of St. John of Jerusalem

As the world grapples with wars and rumors of wars worldwide, people are subjected to enormous pressure, stress and tension in all areas of life thus preventing them from maximizing their true potential and leading an optimal life. The writer of the "Epic Journey from Mediocrity to Greatness," Dr. Debi Prasad Achariya, who started life as a successful banker with many accolades had to give up many initial successes to finally become a seeker of the true happiness and meaning of life thus providing us now with some valuable insights to slow down, ponder and receive the ingredients of joyful living.

He has invited you to explore deeply revealing questions to unearth the hidden value within you. He calls the readers to reflect on these questions and revisit your answers often to remind yourself of your journey and your inherent worth.

He explains how about three decades ago he found himself struggling with adrenal fatigue and an array of chronic health issues, financial woes, and a persistent negative self-image. It seemed he had reached a dead end, far from his aspiration to use his knowledge and skills to aid others, trapped in a cycle of shame and boredom. It was the beginning of his new life!

I am so happy that his quest left him with greater meaning and happiness in life helping him today to live a richer, joyful, authentic life and the ability to communicate such insights for the benefit of mankind. He quotes Milton "The mind is its own place, and in itself can make a heaven of hell, a hell of heaven."

May I say that attitude determines your altitude and with genuine reflection and commitment to shred negative habits, you could lay the foundation of a great life. May the Journey of Mediocrity to Greatness that Debi Prasad Achariya undertook many years ago inspire you and provide you with pearls of wisdom today for your successful journey.

Mr. Ramani Natarajan

Deputy General Manager (Retired), Canara Bank
M. Sc., Postgraduate in Banking Diploma (NIBM, Pune)

The book is remarkable in the sense that it has almost turned out to be a captivating autobiography of the author contrary to my expectation that it would be prosaic prose.

I have known the author for more than four decades, right from the time he was a puny teenager prone to ailments struggling to express himself to his present-day stature. Although one could see the brilliance in his academic pursuits at an early stage, the transformation that came about after he quit his job as a promising officer in a nationalized Bank in his fifties is astounding.

He is now a confident man brimming with confidence and overall well-being.

Over the years, he has acquired expertise in various fields through studies in universities, interaction with eminent mentors, seminars and wide travel.

This book is the culmination of his earnest desire that future generations and people who had come in contact with him should also benefit from his experience and expertise.

What he writes in his book has a ring of truth and practicality since these are his personal experiences.

The style of writing is lucid and keeps the reader engrossed.

Acknowledgements

The core philosophy of this book draws inspiration from luminaries like Joseph Campbell (mythologist), Christopher Vogler (Hollywood screenwriter and author), Bob Proctor (legendary life coach), and Rhonda Byrne ("The Secret" movie).

Being a Mentor of Renatus Wellness, I am also immensely grateful to the "Renatus Retreats," which have allowed me to use those opportunities as my personal learning laboratory. What an indescribable pleasure to meet 3-4 times a year with people throughout India and abroad who are genuinely interested in ideas, who provide constructive critique of any material, suggestion, or practice that comes before them, and who are always eager to test new ideas, new ways of thinking, and new practices.

Finally, I want to thank my wife for tolerating my incessant disappearances into my home office. A lifelong partner makes both the journey and destination worthwhile.

PART I

PRELUDE TO TRANSFORMATION

(CHANGE YOUR PARADIGM TO CHANGE YOUR LIFE)

The Advent of Change

"Without Knowledge, Skill cannot be focused. Without Skill, Strength cannot be brought to bear, and without Strength, Knowledge may not be applied."

~ Alexander the Great

I had everything I thought I wanted and set out to get what I wanted in life. A University topper: gold medallist as a science graduate – and armed with a bank job at a relatively young age... on the surface all looked well, but on the inside, all was not.

Working in a Nationalised Bank in a management position was a great and prestigious assignment with quite a handsome remuneration. Also, with it came a lot of stress and competitiveness, and my boss was not happy with me as I was associated with some intellectual wellness distribution on a part-time basis. However, it helped me to see the world and meet new people with their everyday challenges.

This was a source of great happiness and joy for me as I was able to interact with a greater cross-section of people within the domain of work and outside. Additionally, this venture helped me to overcome my financial crunch, which was like a hidden lesion making me mentally and emotionally upset, besides having perennial physical ailments.

Despite a successful career in banking and accolades in academia, my internal world was in disarray. The prestige of my job masked the stress and dissatisfaction brewing beneath the surface.

One day, my boss asked me about something for which I did not have an answer. He got upset with me and said that after working for 32 long years, I should have gotten it in my head. Eventually, I was placed on a transfer to a remote place, leaving me completely stunned. I realised that my job, despite the prestige and stability it had, was not worth it. This unexpected job transfer was the catalyst that led me to leave my banking career and embark on a path of wellness and self-discovery.

I quit my job at the peak of my career and continued with this wellness distribution. I was very lucky to be mentored by one of the greats in the wellness direct sales industry and got myself associated with numerous eminent personalities in India and abroad.

This marked the beginning of my true education in life - understanding compassion, empathy, and the deeper aspects of human existence. I started seeing real life and tragedies, and joys of everyday existence, and learned the meaning of love and kindness, which had a lot to do with healing.

This ultimately helped me to extend my interest from just marketing wellness products and helping people overcome deficiencies in the larger context of life. I seriously took upon myself learning alternative therapies of healing including the Emotional Freedom Technique (EFT), Qigong Healing Methods, Swar Vigyan, Earthing (Grounding) Techniques, read books which empowered me, attended series of seminars and workshops and till date have been doing just that.

Instead of looking at human beings as a physical machine, where the mechanisms are fixed with sophisticated techniques on account of the evolutions and advancements in the field of medicine, I began to understand the larger context of healing.

Into the Depths – A Profound Turning Point in My Life

After leaving my job at the peak of my career at age 50, I embarked on a new life that embraced healing, alternative therapies, and a profound connection with humanity. Life had a different message for me this time. The process of reconnecting to my emotions and feelings, the melting process of transformation began.

This journey through my abyss taught me the transformative power of releasing old pains and embracing vulnerability.

Over the years, I have been guided by several mentors, each lending a helping hand in their way. However, one piece of advice forever changed my perspective. During a pivotal moment, a mentor confronted me with a question that struck deep: "Why are you always trying to leave the battlefield, man?" This question felt like a heavy blow, forcing me to confront my reality.

I realised then that my usual approach of trying, pushing, grinding, and hustling, was not just ineffective; it was precisely what had led me to this critical point. At that moment, it became clear that there was no way forward but through the "eye of the needle." I needed to venture into territories I had avoided and let go of my preconceptions and fears.

Deciding to stay in the "abyss," I committed to facing whatever came my way. Over the following years, I experienced and surrendered to deep-seated pain, releasing what felt like oceans of suffering. This journey was not about employing old tactics but about embracing vulnerability and transformation.

-15-

The Resurgence: Rediscovering Authenticity and Redefining Life

What I have come to understand is that my deepest wounds were not just scars, but a sanctuary where new beginnings were nurtured. There was a crucial need within me to reconnect with something genuine - a forgotten essence of who I truly was. This period became a time of healing, feeling, and fundamentally altering my worldview. It was a time to envision anew the life I desired and to learn to heed life's deeper calls. My passion for people and transformation needed reigniting, and I sought to uncover my true purpose. It was not long before the currents of life began steering me back to where my journey commenced.

A newfound vigour, confidence, and clarity soon emerged, signalling that I was prepared for the next leg of my journey. As I pen *Epic Journey from Mediocrity to Greatness*, I find myself amidst the swiftest and most transformative growth I have ever known, after two decades as an entrepreneur. The attendance at my seminars and workshops numbers in the thousands, with hundreds more seeking my guidance. This is not mere coincidence – it is a testament to the vital message I must share, one that resonates deeply with others.

This book and the (related) seminar are my gifts to the world, and I am thrilled that you are part of this experience. As we embark on this path together, I hope that the insights you gain will empower you to transition from your current state to where you aspire to be. This could mean building a business, enhancing your health, uncovering unknown facets of yourself, fostering a family, nurturing a community, initiating a movement, or pursuing your passions. This seminar and my book are not about mimicking my journey; they are a canvas for you to sketch your reality, with your true self as the guide.

Radical Responsibility - Intertwining Elements of Philosophical Thought and Motivational Guidance

"It is a painful thing to look at your own trouble and know that you yourself and no one else has made it."

~ Sophocles

Readers are challenged to critically evaluate their lives, the societal constructs they are born into, and the choices they make. By invoking metaphors from the movie "The Matrix," such as choosing between the red pill and the blue pill, it serves as a call to awaken from passive acceptance of life's circumstances and instead embrace a proactive, self-determined approach.

WHICH PILL DO YOU CHOOSE?

THE RED PILL OR THE BLUE PILL?

Most humans on this Earth fail to ever tap into their full potential. This is because, like everyone else on this Earth, we are born into a world of extremely limited possibility (as perceived by most of us).

The narrative contrasts the comfort of conformity with the fulfilment that comes from personal growth and responsibility. It asserts that while many people remain complacent within safe, predefined boundaries, true empowerment and progress come from stepping beyond these limits and taking full ownership of one's actions and their consequences.

The call to action at the end invites the reader to make a formal commitment to this journey of self-realisation and responsibility, emphasising that such a commitment is a personal decision of great significance.

This piece effectively combines motivational rhetoric with philosophical inquiries into the nature of freedom, responsibility, and personal growth, encouraging individuals to not only aspire to adult responsibilities but also to redefine their life stories in more empowering ways.

"Are you aware that 'Matrix' translates to 'Womb'?" This analogy is intriguing, especially when we consider that, unlike the film, many individuals today seem content to remain in a kind of voluntary servitude, their connections to societal norms as binding as an umbilical cord to a nurturing yet controlling parent. This is much like a codependent relationship, where the comfort of familiarity often outweighs the fear of independence. Thus, instead of embracing the thrilling quest of becoming an independent and powerful individual, most settle for the security of a regular income and the distractions of modern technology, which shield them from confronting the deeper, unaddressed voids within.

As I observe the world, I do not see a landscape populated with proactive, empowered adults, but rather a collection of uninitiated children, rarely stepping beyond their familiar realms to engage in life's true adventures. Despite the ongoing degradation of our planet and the increasing entitlement of society, I believe this is not where our story ends. Many are breaking free from this child-like existence.

Having collaborated with hundreds of dedicated, influential individuals and witnessing significant transformations in business and personal contexts, I am optimistic about our collective future. Through seminars and this book, I offer tools not just for personal narrative transformation but also for contributing to humanity's next evolutionary step.

This journey to authentic, impactful adulthood requires embracing full responsibility for your life. Consider this: when a child accidentally breaks a dish, who cleans it up? The adult, of course, because adults take responsibility, something children are yet to learn. Similarly, your strength as an autonomous adult stems from accepting full accountability for your actions. Many resist this, not realising that responsibility is a choice - a liberating one at that. It empowers you to not only shape your future but also reassess and redefine your past.

To be radically responsible is to own up to both your deliberate and subconscious choices. Accepting that your current situation results from past decisions gives you the power to change. If you aspire to evolve into something greater, more authentic, and revitalised, I invite you to embrace total responsibility for your past, present, and future.

Remember, it is adults who take responsibility. I choose to be an adult; I choose to take on challenges and move forward, crafting the reality I envision. I could settle for comfort and safety, but I prefer to lead, not follow. The path you take is yours to choose.

If you are ready to embark on this transformative journey, I invite you not just to follow but to commit to yourself. If you are prepared to leap into the unknown, sign your name here and begin the journey:

Understand Yourself – The Legacy of Alexander the Great

Both in warfare and in business, success typically belongs to those who are not only participants but warriors in their field.

Alexander the Great's domination over Persia was far from an act of blind brutality. It was, instead, the result of clear vision, profound wisdom, and exceptional skills, all driven by a steadfast dedication to a cause greater than any individual, including himself. By the age of 30, he had become the most formidable ruler known in history, a testament to his extraordinary capabilities. Yet, his story takes a poignant turn with his untimely death at 32, the cause of which remains shrouded in mystery - whether from disease or foul play.

Despite his unparalleled leadership and vision, Alexander's path was marred by the harsh realities of relentless conquests that led to widespread devastation and loss of life. The emotional toll of such endeavours must have been immense. Imagine leading a relentless campaign across nearly 3,000 miles, immersed in constant stress, conflict, and chaos. It is plausible that these burdens could precipitate even a robust emperor's premature end.

This leads to a provocative thought: Could it be that Alexander lacked something vital? Historically, warrior cultures like the Macedonians, Greeks, and Spartans embraced a rigid upbringing from a young age, prioritising stoicism - a philosophy born from the necessity to endure the horrors of war. In modern times, as we emerge from millennia of continuous conflict, it seems we might have lost touch with more profound, essential human connections.

Over the years, I have mentored countless entrepreneurs, guiding them to substantial business achievements and, through my experiences, achieving considerable success and influence myself. However, as my professional life expanded, I noticed a growing disconnect from my emotional core.

Fortunately, unlike Alexander, I navigated through this darkness. A pivotal part of my journey was dedicating time to understanding my true self and my needs, which are crucial for thriving, loving, and contributing meaningfully to the world. You are more than just your body or mind; you are a composite of mental, physical, emotional, and archetypal dimensions. Neglecting any of these aspects is akin to living a fragmented, disembodied existence.

To fully realise your potential and steer your destiny, every facet of your being must be engaged and harmonious. This is not merely about designing a life and aggressively pursuing it; it is about a deep, introspective journey to awaken and nurture parts of yourself that have been dormant. The work is vital, as outlined in this stage of *Epic Journey from Mediocrity to Greatness*, ensuring that every aspect is explored.

Whatever lies hidden will be revealed, and what is suppressed will surface; the innate fire within you will be nurtured and amplified. This process is about embracing and embodying what is genuinely yours, ready to be reborn into the world anew.

Discovering Your Life's Purpose

One of my all-time favourite movie scenes comes from "The Lion King." In the story, the kingdom has deteriorated under Scar's tyranny. The once vibrant "Pride Lands" are now a shadow of their former self, shrouded in darkness and despair, with the lions and other animals living in fear.

In a pivotal moment, Nala seeks out Simba, who has forgotten his true nature and shunned his responsibilities in favour of a carefree existence. However, everything changes when Rafiki, the wise and shaman-like baboon, leads Simba to a mysterious lake. There, Simba's reflection transforms into an image of his late father, Mufasa, and in a deeply moving encounter, Simba reconnects with his identity, his father's love, and the daunting destiny awaiting him.

This scene parallels a harsh reality I have observed in entrepreneurship: 96% of businesses fail within their first ten years. This statistic is not just a number; it reflects the intense challenges that come with building and sustaining a business. My experience over 20 years has shown that success often depends on one critical factor - whether a person's business mission is deeply connected to their personal journey.

Why is this connection so vital? Entrepreneurship tests you to your limits. Without a deep commitment to a cause greater than yourself, it is all too easy to retreat to the comfort of what is familiar, just as Simba nearly did. Recognising and embracing your own story, with all its trials and triumphs, is essential.

The struggles you have faced are not only key to your development; they likely lead to profound insights and pivotal shifts in your consciousness. These discoveries are your gifts to the world - your "boon."

In this part of the book, I invite you to explore deeply revealing questions to unearth the hidden value within you. Reflect on these questions and revisit your answers often to remind yourself of your journey and your inherent worth.

Honouring Your Value

Take time to delve into the following questions, write down your responses, and regularly review them to remember your unique value:

- What was the most challenging problem you have faced and overcome?

- What lessons did you learn from that experience?

- What difficult problems can you solve?

- What are the most significant lessons you have learned in your life?

- What extraordinary things have you accomplished?

- What is remarkable about you?

- What values are most important to you?

- Who and what are you most passionate about?

Create a list of your talents and skills, no matter how small or significant, and give yourself permission to celebrate your capabilities. This exercise is not just about self-reflection; it is a crucial step in recognising and embracing the full scope of your personal and professional potential.

What is Holding You Back?

By now, you might have recognised the immense value you possess. The critical question then becomes: are you truly valuing your own worth by sharing your gifts, assisting others, and receiving proper value in return? It is common to see many individuals who fail to fully recognise and leverage their own worth. They often hesitate to embrace their potential, plagued by doubts: Am I capable enough? Can I achieve this? What will others think? Who am I to attempt this?

Such doubts frequently lead to perpetual procrastination, tragically occurring just as one is on the brink of a breakthrough. When faced with obstacles, it is all too easy to unconsciously retreat to what is comfortable and safe rather than pushing forward.

If you neglect the call to fulfil your life's purpose and reveal your true self to the world, you risk falling into a state of depression - the antithesis of expression. This retreat not only stifles your growth but forces you back into playing a lesser version of yourself.

Acknowledging this pattern is the first step towards change. It is essential to understand why you might be holding yourself back. Many people find themselves caught in a chaotic mental state, constantly stressed, or embroiled in drama, without recognising the underlying issue they are avoiding. Addressing and healing these internal conflicts is crucial for achieving a state of non-resistance, embodying flow, and harmony in your life. This journey involves coming out of emotional suppression, releasing trapped emotions, and relearning how to feel - skills that our modern culture often neglects.

If you are ready to move beyond the draining battles of suppressed emotions and embrace a new way that fosters energy, harmony, and health, then there is good news. I will introduce a technique that not only aids in healing and feeling but also helps regulate your nervous system. Ready to dive in?

Let us start with feelings. Like the four primary colours, you have four core emotions: Fear, Anger, Sadness, and Joy. Each emotion is crucial; they provide essential information and serve distinct purposes in your life. Your mission's success fundamentally depends on tapping into these emotions to fuel your actions and creativity.

I describe my approach as "The Modern Warrior" because I believe entrepreneurship involves cultivating a warrior's spirit. A warrior needs access to their anger to set boundaries, make decisions, and effect change. Without this, one is easily swayed by external forces. However, anger is not the only energy a warrior needs.

Consider the deeply profound and often melancholic poetry of ancient Samurai. Your sadness is just as fundamental. It tells you what matters most, connecting you to others and deepening your emotional landscape. Without embracing sadness, one risks becoming unfeeling and disconnected, unable to inspire or move others.

Fear, too, is crucial. Rather than resisting it, understanding and listening to your fear can provide invaluable insights. This acceptance allows a warrior to discern trustworthiness, identify threats, and navigate creative endeavours. Finally, there is joy - the essence of life. Life should be celebrated with laughter, dance, and play.

Embracing all your emotions allows joy to flow naturally. This is the key to effortless action and being in dynamic harmony with your thoughts, feelings, and surroundings. Unfortunately, many spend their lives repressing these essential parts of themselves, leading to a host of problems - physical, emotional, and spiritual. Unravelling these repressions, feelings, and expressing your true emotions is crucial for living a fulfilled life.

Let us now embark on this journey to liberation and authentic expression together.

Defining Your Mission

"He who has a why to live for can bear almost anyhow."

~ Friedrich Nietzsche

- What work are you meant to do?

- Who are your efforts intended to help?

- What message do you wish to share with the world?

- What impact do you aim to create?

Deciding on your mission for the upcoming years is a significant choice. Often, the appeal of safety, security, and comfort can deter us from truly committing to our purpose. To overcome these barriers, the key is to care deeply - about yourself, others, and the world.

Your emotions - anger, sadness, and joy - are vital tools in this journey. I encourage you to harness these feelings to discover what truly matters to you.

Here is an exercise to help clarify your mission, almost like a dragon awakening:

1. Obtain two towels.

2. Stand in a firm horse stance or lie on your back, whichever you prefer.

3. Place one towel in your mouth and begin to twist the other as if it were extremely wet, and you needed to wring it out completely. The objective is to incrementally build your anger from 0% to 100%, if possible.

This may seem absurd or difficult at first, but give it a full three minutes of continuous effort. You might be surprised by the intensity of the emotions that surface, especially if your anger typically feels suppressed.

If finding your anger is challenging, envision someone who consistently irritates you in your mind's eye. As you do this, tell yourself: "I am not angry at them." Your subconscious will likely react - perhaps with a statement like, "I am angry," or even, "I really hate them." Allow whatever arises to manifest, and as you do, clench the towel fiercely. Keep building that anger while repeating, "I am angry because ________________," for three straight minutes.

Once you break through, immediately grab a journal and a pen. Write down everything you feel angry about regarding the world and specific individuals. This raw, unfiltered output is what you are driven to change. Congratulations, you have just identified your mission. Now, it is time to solidify this commitment.

The Vision

"First say to yourself what you would be; and then do what you must do."

~ Epictetus

About three decades ago, I found myself struggling with adrenal fatigue and an array of chronic health issues, financial woes, and a persistent negative self-image. It seemed I had reached a dead end, far from my aspiration to use my knowledge and skills to aid others, trapped in a cycle of shame and boredom.

During this low point, I encountered a wellness venture quite unexpectedly, introducing me to novel ideas about health that seemed to piece together the puzzle of my ailments. A pivotal moment occurred on a flight with my first mentor, where we discussed influential works like Rhonda Byrne's Book and Film "The Secret" and Bob Proctor's "The Science of Getting Rich." Despite their simplicity, these discussions revealed a path I had never imagined, marking the beginning of an incredible transformation.

Previously adrift without direction, I began to understand the importance of having a vision - a "North Star" to navigate through uncharted territories brimming with possibilities. Inspired, I immersed myself in various coaching programmes led by renowned life coaches and mentors, attending sessions that spurred my personal and professional growth.

I committed to crafting a clear vision for my life, dedicating time each morning to visualise my future. This practice, which I maintain to this day, involves imagining myself thriving in transformational settings with large groups or enjoying a fulfilling home life surrounded by a loving family. I envisioned financial independence, allowing myself to truly feel the joy and relief that would come with it.

Remarkably, my adrenal fatigue dissipated. Now, 30 years later, I enjoy reasonably good health, financial stability, and a supportive community of friends and followers, all results of my decision to leave my conventional job and embark on what I call my "Wellness Mission," aptly named "Success Life Creation" with the motto "Unlock Potentials - Expand Possibilities."

This journey underscores the power of a vision. It is the seed from which all growth springs. Now, I encourage you to reflect on your future:

- Where do you see yourself?
- Who are you with?
- How are you spending your days?
- What is your professional life like?
- What achievements have you accomplished in your work and personal life?
- How do your friends and family view and speak of you?

Dream boldly, for as Alexander the Great once proclaimed, "There is nothing impossible to him who will try."

Ignorance versus Knowledge

"Most people who are highly successful have unconscious competence. They cannot articulate why they are doing so well."

~ Legendary Late Bob Proctor

Bob Proctor, the revered figure, once observed that many highly successful individuals operate on "unconscious competence," meaning they excel without fully understanding why. He attributed this phenomenon to the influence of deeply ingrained paradigms - fixed ideas in our subconscious that guide our actions without our conscious awareness. Proctor emphasised that success hinges more on our internal mindset than external circumstances.

This concept became particularly evident during the challenging times of the pandemic. While many faced financial hardship and job losses, others thrived, not merely through positive thinking, but by shifting their paradigms. Such shifts involve changing the fundamental habits that operate subconsciously, like driving a car without conscious thought, thanks to ingrained programming.

Life can follow two distinct paths: ignorance and knowledge. The path of ignorance is fraught with worry, doubt, fear, anxiety, depression, disease, and ultimately disintegration. Ignorance stems from a lack of knowledge, yet knowledge is universally accessible, eliminating any need to remain ignorant. Unfortunately, traditional education systems fall short in teaching how to manage our minds, respond instead of reacting, maintain a positive mindset, or understand universal laws and paradigms.

The journey often begins with ignorance and worry at the conscious level, which seeps into the subconscious, manifesting as fear. This fear vibrates through the body, creating anxiety that is typically suppressed, leading to depression and eventually disease.

In contrast, the path of knowledge represents a positive trajectory. While knowledge is readily available in libraries and online, it alone does not equate to power. If it did, librarians would be among the wealthiest. Instead, knowledge must be organised and directed intelligently to be truly powerful. Without a paradigm shift, even the hardest work and longest hours will fail to yield significant, lasting success.

At "Success Life Creation," we have dedicated the last 15 years to organising and directing knowledge towards creating a world filled with power, possibility, and promise.

Success Life Creation

(Shape Your Destiny with Your Mind)

"Success Life Creation" is more than just a name; it is a powerful philosophy that can transform your life. The essence of this philosophy lies in the belief that you have the power to shape your destiny through the thoughts you hold and the actions you take. By harnessing the power of your mind, you can create the success you desire in every aspect of your life.

Imagine your life as an orchestra. Just as every musician and instrument plays an essential role in creating a perfect melody, each aspect of your life contributes to your overall harmony.

This is the concept of "Harmonic Wealth."

Harmonic Wealth is not just limited to material abundance - though that is fun and necessary - but encompasses wealth in every area of life. Would you not want every part of your life moving towards an elegant whole, greater than the sum of its parts? That is what Harmonic Wealth is all about.

You can achieve financial security, profound relationships, clear thoughts, a healthy body, and spiritual peace. This is the essence of "Success Life Creation."

Redefining Wealth

Most people equate wealth with money. While money is an integral part of wealth, true wealth is a state of harmony and well-being. It includes abundance in every area of life: physical, intellectual, emotional, financial, social, spiritual, occupational, and environmental. You achieve Harmonic Wealth when your thoughts, feelings, and actions are perfectly aligned. Without this harmony, you may be rich, but not truly wealthy.

Think of that orchestra once again. Not all instruments play at once. Sometimes the saxophone leads, other times it is the bass, the drums, or the lead guitar. Regardless of which instrument leads, each one contributes to creating a beautiful, rhythmic melody. Similarly, in your life, sometimes your parenting skills will take the lead, while other times your job or business will. There will be moments when your marriage takes centre stage. The key is to maintain harmony.

The Newtonian and Quantum Realms

We live in a consumer-driven world and are familiar with Newtonian Physics, which involves direct cause and effect, linear thinking, and a mechanistic approach to the three-dimensional world. However, there is another realm - the "Quantum Realm." It is non-linear, holographic, and operates on subtle energy. To achieve true Harmonic Wealth, you must learn to operate in both realms simultaneously. Respect the linear Newtonian results visible while acknowledging the non-linear quantum level.

The Power of the Mind

"The mind is its own place, and in itself can make a heaven of hell, a hell of heaven."

~ John Milton

Neuroscientists tell us that 95% of our thoughts are controlled by our subconscious mind, which operates based on preprogrammed patterns from our past experiences. This means that many of us are reliving old stories and limiting beliefs, which hold us back from achieving our true potential. To break free from this cycle, we need to consciously create new neural pathways and adopt a mindset of growth and possibility.

Everything that comes into your life is attracted by the images you hold in your mind. Your thoughts create an attractive force that governs your life's outcomes. To live an extraordinary life, you must develop mental strength and willpower. This mental faculty allows you to focus on one idea to the exclusion of all distractions.

Great achievers of the past were visionary figures. They imagined what could be, rather than what already was, and took action to make it a reality. Your vision is invaluable in the process of life success. If you can conceive it in your mind, you can bring it into the physical world. The first step is to predict your successful future.

Real-Life Examples

1. **The Wright Brothers**: Orville and Wilbur Wright, the pioneers of aviation, did not accept the common belief that human flight was impossible. Instead, they visualised their success and worked tirelessly towards their goal. By challenging the status quo and believing in their vision, they created one of the most significant breakthroughs in history.

2. **Oprah Winfrey**: Coming from a background of poverty and abuse, Oprah Winfrey used the power of her mind to envision a better future. She focused on her goals, worked hard, and overcame numerous obstacles to become one of the most influential media moguls in the world.

3. **Jim Carrey**: Before he became a famous actor, Jim Carrey was a struggling artist. He wrote himself a check for $10 million for "acting services rendered" and dated it five years in the future. Carrey visualised himself achieving his dream, and within that timeframe, he received a movie role that paid him exactly that amount.

Taking Action

Do not worry about how you will achieve your goals or where the resources will come from. Your job is to identify the "what." Power your decisions with enthusiasm and recharge them daily by focusing on your life board visions. Refuse to worry about the "how." Use your mental imagery to freeze-frame your vision with intention and activate it with decision. Become the star of your life's movie, not just an extra.

The Journey with "Success Life Creation"

As you begin your journey with "Success Life Creation," remember that your time is now. No matter your circumstances, you can bring positive changes into your life. We will explore powerful personal development tools, techniques, and strategies to help you attract everything you desire through your thoughts and actions.

You may have already experienced some of these techniques and dismissed the results as luck, miracles, or just being in the right place at the right time. This journey is not religious but explores the mind-body-spirit relationship and how inner insight and intention manifest your visions in the outer world. It is about today and now. Suspend your disbelief and believe that anything is possible in your life by embracing change. Be brave and take the leap - what comes next will amaze you.

For those interested in this journey, I invite you to follow the channels listed at the end of this book.

PART II

HOW TO FIND YOUR "LIFE PURPOSE" – THE ROLE OF "FATE AND DESTINY"

"The mystery of human existence lies not in just staying alive, but in finding something to live for."

~ Fyodor Dostoyevsky

Finding your life purpose is one of the most fulfilling journeys you can embark upon. It involves understanding your passions, strengths, and the unique impact you can make in the world. Fate and destiny play significant roles in this process, guiding you towards paths that align with your intrinsic nature and desires. This chapter explores the importance of finding your life's purpose and why seeking your life's purpose is essential. It will offer a solution to overcome obstacles in your path and then discover and actualise your destiny.

What Is My Purpose?

"The purpose of life is not to be happy. It is to be useful, to be honourable, to be compassionate, to have it make some difference that you have lived and lived well."

~ Ralph Waldo Emerson

Your purpose is the reason you get up in the morning; it is the driving force that makes life meaningful and fulfilling. It is not just about what you do for a living, but about what truly matters to you and how you want to contribute to the world.

Your purpose is the essence that defines who you are and directs your life's choices. It is the central theme of your existence that aligns with your deepest values and passions. Understanding your purpose gives every action more meaning and clarity.

Why Seeking Your Life's Purpose Is Essential?

"Your purpose in life is to find your purpose and give your whole heart and soul to it."

~ Buddha

Engaging in the pursuit of your life's purpose is vital because it contributes significantly to your overall happiness and satisfaction. A life driven by purpose feels more fulfilling and enriching than one lived without direction.

When you understand your purpose, you can align your actions and decisions with your core values, leading to a more satisfying and impactful life.

Overcoming Obstacles to Finding Your Purpose

"The only limit to our realisation of tomorrow will be our doubts of today."

~ Franklin D. Roosevelt

Identifying your purpose can be challenging with distractions and pressures from society. Overcoming these obstacles involves self-reflection, resilience, and sometimes, seeking guidance from mentors or coaches.

It requires introspection, the courage to face your fears, and the resilience to overcome failures. Each obstacle is a stepping stone towards clearer understanding.

Knowing Your Purpose and Why It Matters

"Efforts and courage are not enough without purpose and direction."

~ John F. Kennedy

Knowing your purpose helps in making decisions that are congruent with your true self. It provides a compass in times of uncertainty and motivates you to persevere through hardships.

Knowing your purpose matters because it shapes your identity and influences how you interact with the world. It helps you prioritise your time and energy on things that truly matter, fostering a sense of fulfilment and contentment.

Putting Your Purpose into Action

"The purpose of life is not to be happy. It is to be useful, to be honorable, to be compassionate, to have it make some difference that you have lived and lived well."

~ Ralph Waldo Emerson

Once you have identified your purpose, it is crucial to put it into action. This involves setting goals aligned with your purpose and taking consistent steps towards achieving them.

It is about integrating your purpose into every aspect of your life.

Steps to Discover Your Purpose in Life

1. Understand Where You Are Now

"Knowing yourself is the beginning of all wisdom."

~ Aristotle

Start by assessing your current situation - your feelings, accomplishments, and dissatisfaction. Understanding your starting point is essential in charting your course towards your purpose. This self-awareness is the foundation of your journey.

2. Focus on Purpose-Driven Goals Rather Than Short-Term Goals

"The key to success is to focus our conscious mind on things we desire, not things we fear."

~ Brian Tracy

Aim for goals that align with your long-term purpose rather than immediate, short-term gains. This ensures sustained motivation and fulfilment.

Long-term, purpose-driven goals provide a blueprint for meaningful success, while short-term goals are merely steps along the path.

3. Cultivate an Abundance Mindset

"When you realize there is nothing lacking, the whole world belongs to you."

~ Lao Tzu

Embrace a mindset that believes in unlimited possibilities and opportunities. This perspective allows you to pursue your purpose without fear of scarcity.

Believe that there is enough success, love, and creativity to go around. This mindset will open opportunities and attract resources.

4. Give to Something Bigger Than Yourself

"The best way to find yourself is to lose yourself in the service of others."

~ Unknown

Engage in activities that contribute to the greater good. This not only helps others, but also enriches your sense of purpose.

Contributing to a cause greater than oneself can provide clarity and a sense of belonging.

5. Throw Out Your Blueprint and Choose What You Want

"Your work is to discover your work and then, with all your heart, to give yourself to it."

~ Buddha

Discard preconceived notions of what your life should be like. Create your own path based on your true desires and passions.

Release preconceived notions of success and happiness. Forge a path that truly resonates with your inner self.

6. Think About What Brings You Joy

"Success is not the key to happiness. Happiness is the key to success. If you love what you are doing, you will be successful."

~ Albert Schweitzer

Reflect on activities that make you lose track of time and make you happy and energised. These are often clues to your true purpose and passions.

7. Find Your Gift

"Your talent is God's gift to you. What you do with it is your gift back to God."

~ Leo Buscaglia

Recognise your unique talents and skills. These gifts are integral to your purpose and how you can make a difference. Identifying yours can guide you to your purpose.

8. Write Your Story

"Your life is your story. Write well. Edit often."

~ Unknown

Document your journey, including your aspirations, challenges, and achievements. This narrative helps clarify your purpose and track your progress.

Imagine the narrative of your ideal life. Writing it down makes it more tangible and achievable.

9. Visualise Your Future

"The future belongs to those who believe in the beauty of their dreams."

~ Eleanor Roosevelt

Use visualisation to manifest your aspirations. Seeing your goals clearly can motivate you to act towards them. Imagine where you want to be in the future and how you want to feel.

10. Discover Your True Needs

"Knowing your own darkness is the best method for dealing with the darkness of other people."

~ Carl Jung

Understand your core needs and how they influence your choices and behaviours. Differentiate between what you want and what you truly need.

Focusing on essential needs can simplify living a purposeful life.

11. Take Time for Yourself

"Almost everything will work again if you unplug it for a few minutes, including you."

~ Anne Lamott

Allocate time for self-reflection and self-care, for solitude and meditation. Self-reflection is crucial in understanding your desires and motivations. This helps you stay connected to your purpose and prevents burnout.

12. Practice Self-Compassion

"You yourself, as much as anybody in the entire universe, deserve your love and affection."

~ Buddha

Be kind to yourself during the journey. Understand that finding your purpose is a process and accept that mistakes are part of learning and growth.

13. Build Your Community

"Surround yourself with only people who are going to lift you higher."

~ Oprah Winfrey

Surround yourself with supportive and like-minded individuals who encourage you to pursue your purpose. A strong community provides strength and inspiration.

Finding your life purpose is a transformative journey that requires introspection, resilience, and action. By understanding your purpose, you align your life with your deepest values and passions, leading to a fulfilling and impactful existence.

By following these steps and embracing the role of fate and destiny, you can align your actions with your deepest values and aspirations, leading to a fulfilling and purpose-driven life.

This is a guide supported by timeless wisdom for discovering and living your purpose, to inspire and guide you along the way.

"If you can't figure out your purpose, figure out your passion. For your passion will lead you right into your purpose."

~ Bishop T.D. Jakes

PART III

UNEARTHING YOUR UNIQUE CALLING AND FULFILLING YOUR EARTHLY PURPOSE

Welcome to Planet Earth!

Imagine possessing a map that could guide you from your current situation to the most extraordinary, fulfilling, and spectacular life imaginable. A map that details every step required to achieve your grandest dreams, navigate through obstacles, and conquer challenges against all odds. You now hold that map in your hands - your personal guide to greatness.

This book is dedicated to helping you find your purpose, regardless of your current stage in life or your age. It is never too late to pursue your dreams.

You possess a unique quality, something you were born to achieve and embody, which none of the billions of others can replicate. You have a distinct life destined for you - a path only you can follow.

With the invaluable insights you are about to gain from this book, coupled with your innate abilities, you are equipped to realise your dreams and discover the profound, enduring happiness we all seek.

The Call to Adventure

Planet Earth presents an exquisitely beautiful setting, adorned with vast oceans, towering mountains, lush jungles, breathtaking coastlines, expansive plains, and a diverse array of spectacular animals and creatures. Amidst this natural splendour, humans experience profound joy.

However, life on Earth also poses significant challenges. Growth is often painful, encompassing stages from childhood through old age, accompanied by physical suffering, poverty, grief, and the inevitability of death. This duality of joy and suffering defines our world - a realm of opposites where light and darkness, warmth and cold, joy and despair coexist.

In this world, relationships fluctuate between love and estrangement, security gives way to uncertainty, and wealth may turn into poverty. Every human embodies both positive and negative traits, reflecting the inherent contrasts of our existence.

You are here to navigate the adventure of life in this stunning yet demanding environment. Fortunately, you are equipped with remarkable abilities to realise your dreams and surmount the obstacles you will face. Yet, being born into the constraints of the material world means your mind and consciousness are limited, causing you to forget your true nature and the strengths within.

Remember, no one is born into a perfect life. Without challenges, there would be no impetus to strive, create, or dream. Regardless of whether you were born in India, the US, or anywhere else, your initial circumstances do not define your destiny. You possess every necessary quality to fulfil your dreams and achieve whatever you desire, regardless of the odds.

Against All Odds

Life's toughest circumstances and overwhelming odds often serve as catalysts, propelling us toward discovering and pursuing our dreams. Success is not determined by any external conditions - your financial status, educational background, social connections, or prior experience. Instead, it hinges on recognising and utilising the inner abilities you possess to navigate and conquer the challenges you encounter in the outside world. This approach is common among successful individuals, and it is a path you can follow as well.

By pursuing your dreams, you unearth the greatness within yourself. True greatness is not about being born into privilege; it is about recognising the Hero within and embracing your aspirations.

What is Your Calling?

Every individual born, past, present, or future, is endowed with a unique talent or ability; we call it a calling. While every person possesses this intrinsic quality, many go through life without ever recognising or embracing it.

Your calling is what deeply moves and excites you, something towards which you feel a strong passion. It is what fills you with joy and ignites your heart when you engage in it. This could manifest as a burning ambition in business, sports, your profession, or even a hobby. Often, hobbies provide insights into our callings because they represent what we are passionate about and willingly dedicate time to pursue. Many successful enterprises have originated from such hobbies.

Your calling might also be a long-held dream about a particular way of life or achievement that seems unattainable. Yet, when you contemplate this dream, you experience profound happiness and fulfilment. Regardless of how unreachable the dream may appear, the deep-seated urge to follow it is your true calling.

Purpose of Your Existence on this Planet

Throughout your life, whether you are aware of it or not, you have received messages from your subconscious - a calling that has echoed within your own self multiple times. Perhaps as a child, you had a clear vision of what you wanted to become when you grew up. However, societal pressures or well-intentioned guidance from parents and teachers often present us with a narrow view of what is achievable, causing many to suppress their true calling and dreams.

The call might have also come during what seemed like a mundane moment - something you saw, read, or heard suddenly striking you like a bolt of lightning, transforming an ordinary instant into a pivotal moment of your life.

Remember, no circumstance in life is entirely negative. Every challenge holds a seed of its opposite, meaning there is something beneficial hidden within every adverse situation. Life is not about the negative experiences that occur but about how you leverage the golden opportunities that lie within those experiences.

You are never compelled to pursue a dream without having multiple avenues to realise it. It is fundamentally impossible to dream of something if, at the very least, the essence of that dream cannot be actualised. Your dreams are not just fantasies; they are calls to action – invitations to lead the best life possible and to discover the Hero within yourself.

My Call to Adventure

Embracing new experiences with flexibility, curiosity, and creativity activates your mind and opens you up to endless possibilities and opportunities. The path these opportunities take you on can be unpredictable and profoundly transformative.

I often speak of synchro-destiny - those serendipitous moments that seem like mere coincidences but actually guide us toward unforeseen possibilities. When we venture into the universe with openness, we invite synchro-destiny, paving the way for our desires to manifest.

Coincidences are not random; they are manifestations of synchronicity. They occur when we align ourselves with the myriad possibilities available to us. However, our openness can sometimes be clouded by underlying ego issues that need to be acknowledged and addressed.

Consider this: divine intelligence permeates every atom and subatomic particle in the universe, infusing everything with inherent wisdom. Our lives are a continuous game of hide and seek with our divinity, mingling fear, excitement, and thrill. We are called to experience what divinity truly is, to let it "catch" us and strip away the veils of ego. We often fear realising our dreams - what if they do come true? Dreams make us feel invincible, yet we often retract from them, stepping out of our dream state only to withdraw again. In doing so, we miss the synchronistic coincidences that could lead us toward our true paths.

Coincidences - synchronistic events that occur in harmony and cooperation - do not happen by chance but are purposeful and constant.

Miracles, often perceived as large, earth-shaking events, are actually the smallest occurrences that unfold daily. We frequently overlook these miracles, recognising them only in retrospect because we are too caught up in the physical realm.

Ignoring the call to adventure out of fear or disbelief might lead to circumstances that push you towards your dreams, as I recounted in Chapter I. Obstacles can reveal deeper passions and expand our vision. What seems like a negative outcome can often be the catalyst for growth and transformative experiences.

For some, the call comes early, but I remain thankful for that "transfer order" in my previous job which compelled me to pursue my dreams at a later stage in life. This opportunity was a crucial turning point, allowing me to embark on the most exhilarating and fulfilling journey of my life.

Refusal of the Call

Laird Hamilton starkly warns, "The risk that you take in not pursuing your dream is terminal. It is the end. It is a life without fulfilment; it is a life without accomplishment; it is a life without contentment, and it is a life without joy. It is misery."

Choosing to follow your dreams is a straightforward path; ignoring this calling, however, is fraught with difficulty. By refusing the call, you risk a life marred by misery, devoid of joy, passion, and ultimately, purpose.

G. M. Rao reflects on the consequences of ignoring your passions: "When you don't follow your dream or passion, then what you work for will seem like a cage, albeit a golden one. Body without soul! It will result in being frustrated, listless, and completely devoid of a purpose for existence."

Life is Not a Dress Rehearsal

It is easy to think, "I have time to follow my dreams." But realistically, you do not have that time. Life is fleeting. The average life expectancy translates to about 71 years - or 25,915 days. Whether we live more days or fewer, each one is precious and finite, so delaying your dreams is not an option. It is now or never. Procrastination will only lead to unfulfilled potential and lifelong regrets. The time to act is now.

Michael Acton Smith puts it vividly: "Life is short; it's not a dress rehearsal. It's about grabbing it by the scruff of the neck and experiencing as many things and meeting as many people as possible. It is definitely not about sitting on the sofa, watching TV, and moaning about what might have been."

"Someday" is a Disease

Timothy Ferriss, author of "The 4-Hour Workweek," starkly warns that "Someday" is a disease that will carry your dreams to the grave with you.

Understanding that no one else can fulfil your dreams for you is crucial. Neither your boss, friends, partner, family, nor children can live your life for you. It is solely your responsibility to create a life that brings you happiness and fulfilment.

Laird Hamilton echoes a similar sentiment, "The fear of failure stops people from doing a lot of things. My mom used to have a saying that we are each our greatest inhibitors - that we stop ourselves."

Despite naysayers proclaiming that all great opportunities are gone, the world is in constant flux, offering new opportunities at every turn.

The Illusion of Security

Do not let the pursuit of money and security dictate your life choices. Life is inherently unstable; companies fail, jobs are lost, and personal circumstances like divorce or health issues can disrupt what seemed like a secure life. Security is often an illusion, trapping even those who are financially well-off but find their work unfulfilling and their lives joyless.

While material wealth can enhance life's pleasures, societal conditioning often misleads us into believing that accumulating possessions is life's primary goal. Avoid reaching the end of your life filled with regret over ventures that are not attempted. Your life is invaluable, and true happiness stems from pursuing your dreams, not settling for perceived security.

Do not wait for a breaking point to initiate change. Start now. Even if you feel ensnared by security and obligations, it is never too late to pursue your dreams. There are always myriad ways to follow your passions, and it is easier than you might think.

Finding Your Dream

Release the opinions, beliefs, and conclusions you hold about yourself, as these are often barriers that prevent you from realising your true potential. Avoid comparing yourself to others; you possess unique potential that no one else on Earth has. Discard the self-limiting thoughts about what is possible for you and open your mind to all possibilities.

Imagine waking up each morning as if it were the first day of your life, with a clean slate. Every possibility would be open to you without the burdens of past baggage. Ask yourself: What would you do if you could do anything? What would you pursue if money were not a consideration? What would you attempt if you knew you could not fail? When you genuinely seek answers to these questions about your purpose, the Universe will provide them, not through your conscious mind - which would already know - but from the universal consciousness.

Follow Your Bliss

Joseph Campbell, the highly esteemed mythologist, taught us a simple yet profound principle: "Follow Your Bliss." This directive serves as a compass, guiding you towards what brings you joy in every decision. Bliss is the deep joy and fulfilment you experience when engaging in what you love, a direct line to your dreams.

Consider the amount of time spent at work: if you are like most of the population, it is about 250 days per year. This accounts for over two-thirds of your time annually. If your job does not ignite your passion, excite you, or make your heart sing, then you are not just losing days – you are missing out on a significant portion of your life.

Warren Buffett wisely advises, "Take a job that you love. I think you are out of your mind if you keep taking jobs that you don't like because you think it will look good on your resume. Isn't that a little like saving up sex for your old age?" This illustrates the absurdity of postponing what brings you joy in pursuit of superficial gains.

Vision

"Success is achieved twice. Once in the mind and the second time in the real world," Azim Premji famously stated.

Mastering the art of visualising the outcome of your dreams as if they have already transpired is essential. This powerful technique can also be applied to smaller steps or goals along your journey. Even if you only visualise the result of what you desire, your vision ensures that you will reach your destination, one way or another.

Visualisation can be used for any situation in which you wish to succeed. Imagine achieving the best outcomes in exams, auditions, interviews, meetings, trips, or even receiving the largest raise in your company's history. Observe the transformations in your life when you apply this practice.

Sara Blakely advises, "You've got to visualize where you're headed and be very clear about it. Take a Polaroid picture of where you're going to be in a few years."

Something Good is Just About to Happen

Peter Burwash once described two neighbours: one who opens his window in the morning and exclaims, "Good morning, God!" while the other, a pessimist, groans, "Good God, it's morning."

Reflect on whether blaming and complaining could ever turn someone's life into a story of success and happiness. Do you believe that whining and criticising can fulfil someone's dreams and bring them everlasting happiness?

Consider the demeanour of film icons like Superman, Indiana Jones, and James Bond. These characters do not engage in blaming, whining, or complaining because such traits would diminish their heroic stature, making them less admirable to the audience. The essence here is clear: negativity cannot coexist with heroism.

Blame, resentment, whining, and complaining are merely excuses for not living the fulfilling life we are destined to lead.

Fear as a Catalyst for Evolution

Fear is an intrinsic emotion that has been pivotal in human evolution.

Mastin Kipp encapsulates this notion beautifully, saying, "There is a great book called 'Feel the Fear and Do It Anyway.' I read the title, and that's all I read. I didn't need to read the rest of the book; I got it. And that's really the best advice."

This idea is vividly portrayed in fantasy movies, where Heroes confront dragons or monsters - symbols of the fears and doubts that plague our minds. These cinematic quests mirror our own life challenges, emphasising that overcoming fear is essential to achieving our dreams. No matter the size of the dream, stepping outside one's comfort zone involves facing fear, a fundamental aspect of self-preservation and growth.

The Power of Intuition

"Have the courage to follow your heart and intuition. They somehow already know what you truly want to become," Steve Jobs famously advised.

Intuition strikes with a strong, compelling feeling, guiding us decisively in moments of uncertainty. Often, people second-guess this profound internal communication, allowing rational thoughts to override these intuitive impulses.

Ancient teachings suggest that intuition is a form of knowledge from a higher consciousness, transmitted to us through vibrations that the subconscious mind and endocrine glands decode into feelings or impressions. This intuitive knowledge often manifests as sensations in the stomach or around the heart, signalling guidance from the Universal Mind.

Mastin Kipp asserts, "Intuition is the primary tool you need to make your dream a reality. Without trusting your intuition, you are going to fall flat over and over again."

Trusting this communication is crucial, despite any seemingly contradictory evidence.

The Golden Rule

Roger Federer once said, "It's nice to be important, but it's more important to be nice."

This sentiment captures the essence of the "Golden Rule" and its profound impact on achieving true happiness. Treating others poorly disrupts our connection to the collective human family and the Universe itself, leading to negative consequences.

Conversely, kindness, even in challenging situations, attracts positive outcomes, opportunities, and what some might call "lucky breaks."

Tom Shadyac, a film director, relates this to Newton's third law of motion or karma, emphasising that the energy you put into the world - good or bad - ultimately returns to you. This cause-and-effect principle, or the idea that "the fruit is in the seed," illustrates that our actions and behaviours shape the outcomes of our lives.

Commitment – "The Time is Now"

Mastin Kipp highlights the importance of commitment in realising your dreams: "If you make a full commitment to your dream, doors will open."

Often, we delay actions waiting for the perfect moment or the last crucial element we think we need. However, the right time is not in some indefinite future; it is the present moment. Commitment acts as a key, revealing opportunities and pathways that were always there but unseen. This decisive moment of commitment signals to the Universe your readiness, aligning you with guides and mentors - embodied by the adage, "when the student is ready, the teacher appears."

By committing fully to your aspirations, you transform potential barriers into gateways.

Commitment and the Universe

Often, when we witness someone pursuing their dreams, it is easy to assume they had inherent privileges. However, the reality is usually the reverse: privileges and opportunities often emerge because of taking decisive action towards a dream.

The Universe has a way of aligning the right circumstances or people at just the right moment, but this only happens when there is a firm commitment to the dream. If you entertain a backup plan (Plan B), your focus divides, potentially leading your subconscious to settle for the lesser option.

To truly realise your dreams, you must invest fully in Plan A – pour all your love, faith, energy, and determination into it. This undivided focus ensures that it is Plan A that materialises, not just a fallback.

Never, Never, Never Give Up

Pete Carroll encapsulates a vital attitude towards life and dreams: "If you feel that you're done, then you are, because that's hopeless. We don't want to ever get to the point where we're totally hopeless. There is always hope. To me, something good is going to come your way."

Life is inherently dualistic; it is filled with highs and lows. Everyone has days where everything feels like a struggle, as if moving through mud. Yet, there are also days when everything clicks, you feel on top of the world, and anything seems achievable. These are moments filled with joy and powerful emotions, fuelling a sense of invincibility.

The key is to chase that joy, follow your bliss, and that energy will provide the determination needed to achieve your dreams.

The Labyrinth of Dreams

The journey towards your dreams is rarely straightforward. You might start with a clear destination in mind, but the path to get there is often unknown.

Like navigating a labyrinth, you can only see a few feet ahead, discovering the route as you go. Each twist and turn reveals a little more of the path, and along the way, you may encounter dead ends or unexpected shortcuts that propel you forward.

The journey of those you admire - those who inspire you - also began without knowing exactly how they would achieve their dreams. They had aspirations and intentions, but the exact path was revealed through the adventure of the journey itself.

One Step at a Time

As you pursue your dreams, it is important to remember to take things one step at a time. It is the only way you can really move forward. Regardless of your current circumstances, there is always a step you can take.

Looking back after achieving your dreams, you will often see that what seemed like obstacles were pivotal moments that redirected you towards an even better realisation of your dreams than you had imagined. What appear to be walls or dead ends are merely illusions, detours that guide you to a greater version of your aspirations.

Mastin Kipp, reflecting on the entrepreneurial mindset, describes this process as pivoting: "If it doesn't work, I'm going to pivot - implement what I learned and come up with something new." This philosophy encapsulates the essence of the Hero's Journey - continuously adapting, learning, and persevering until you achieve your goals.

Naysayers and New Paths

Howard Schultz, Chairman and CEO of Starbucks, once remarked, "So many times, I have been told that it can't be done. Again and again, I've had to use every ounce of perseverance to make it happen."

Naysayers often seem like obstacles on your path, but they can inadvertently guide you towards a better route. You may have a specific vision for how your dream should unfold, but encountering naysayers, particularly those in positions of power, can halt your progress. This forced pause pushes you to find an alternative route that often turns out to be superior to your original plan.

In a way, these naysayers, by challenging your path, bless you with the opportunity to discover a more fruitful one.

Ignore the Trivial Many

Mark Twain wisely advised, "Keep away from people who try to belittle your ambitions. Small people always do that, but the really great make you feel that you, too, can become great."

It is crucial to foster self-belief and conviction in your dream before sharing it broadly. Prematurely discussing your aspirations can lead to discouragement from others, potentially causing you to abandon your goals before they are fully formed.

Imagine having a brilliant idea outside your usual expertise, sharing it, and being filled with doubt by others, only to later see someone else achieve great success with a similar concept.

This scenario underscores the importance of selecting who you share your dreams with and reinforcing your own commitment to them before seeking external validation.

Allies on Your Journey

Layne Beachley, a champion surfer, once emphasised, "All successful people have achieved by standing on the shoulders of others, and it's important, no matter how successful you are, that you remember and realise who has helped you along in this journey."

As you pursue your dreams, it is inevitable that you will encounter naysayers, but equally, you will meet numerous allies. These allies, whether they have been in your lifelong term or appear momentarily, are crucial in supporting and aiding your progress.

Achieving a dream is never a solitary effort. Along your path, you will find many individuals eager to assist and propel you forward. The support can come from unexpected quarters - people you know well or those you might have just met. The moments when someone steps up to help, often when you least expect it, are among the most heartening and surprising aspects of any journey towards a dream.

The Road of Trials and Miracles

Peter Burwash articulates a fundamental truth about human experience: "Every day has hurdles. There's nobody who wakes up in the morning without something wrong physically, mentally, emotionally, or spiritually. Accept the fact that you're going to have hurdles. Everybody has them. People say, 'Why me?' Why not you?".

This perspective encourages embracing challenges as part of the journey, rather than seeing them as unusual or unfairly targeted at oneself.

Similarly, Derek Jeter, an American baseball champion, reinforces this mindset: "The path to your goal is not always going to be smooth. Obstacles will arise and problems will develop, but you must remember what you're striving for... don't forget the big picture and don't let small mishaps or small failures stop you."

This advice highlights the importance of maintaining focus on the ultimate goal and not being deterred by the inevitable setbacks that occur. Together, these insights underline the essence of perseverance and maintaining perspective amid the trials that accompany any meaningful endeavour.

Challenges and Obstacles

G.M. Rao, reflecting on his experiences, once said, "The course of my journey in business has been like the flow of a river, where each obstacle made me change course, eventually to reach my destination. All my life has been full of challenges. Each challenge was a meaningful coincidence and opened a door to a bigger opportunity."

This perspective highlights that every obstacle or challenge on the Hero's Journey serves as a catalyst for personal growth, building strength of character and honing the necessary qualities and abilities to overcome these hurdles. Importantly, the magnitude of the obstacles faced often correlates with the size of potential successes, bringing you closer to your goals.

Overcoming challenges not only bolsters self-confidence but also deepens faith in oneself and in the divine, equipping you for even greater endeavours.

Failures and Mistakes

Layne Beachley views mistakes as integral learning opportunities, stating, "Mistakes are really a learning opportunity, and the only mistake is not learning the lesson the first time. And the great thing about the Universe is it'll keep providing you with the same lesson until you learn it."

Embracing responsibility for failures and mistakes, rather than assigning blame, transforms these experiences into valuable lessons that propel you forward on the Hero's Journey. Mistakes are inevitable, but the wisdom they impart is a choice.

Echoing this sentiment, Warren Buffett shares, "We make mistakes. It wouldn't be any fun if we didn't make mistakes. If I went out and played golf and every one of the eighteen holes, I hit a hole in one, I wouldn't be playing golf for a long time; I mean, you have to go into the rough occasionally to make the game interesting. Not too often though."

This analogy underlines the importance of challenges in maintaining interest and growth in any endeavour.

The Supreme Ordeal

Jim Carrey poignantly captures the essence of determination in his statement, "It is better to risk starving to death than surrender. If you give up on your dreams, what's left?"

In the narrative arc of The Hero's Journey by Joseph Campbell, this sentiment heralds the approach of the Supreme Ordeal - a formidable challenge that precedes the achievement of success.

This critical phase often seems like the potential death of your dream but is in fact a precursor to its realisation. In cinematic terms, this is seen when the Hero, having surmounted numerous obstacles, faces a final, near-insurmountable challenge just as victory (be it rescuing the princess or seizing the Holy Grail) is within grasp.

Paul Orfalea echoes a similar sentiment with the Chinese proverb: "Crisis is Opportunity." This reflects the idea that within every setback lies the potential for a significant breakthrough.

The Reward

The culmination of overcoming the "Supreme Ordeal" is not merely the end but the onset of a new chapter filled with opportunities and financial rewards. These successes bring a profound sense of freedom and are often accompanied by a rush of opportunities to expand and enhance your original dream. However, the true value of these achievements is not found solely in material gains but in the immense joy and satisfaction derived from accomplishing what once seemed impossible.

This emotional peak is akin to the elation experienced by athletes at the moment of winning gold medals or breaking records. The intense energy and jubilation not only affect the spectators, stirring exhilaration and even tears, but are also profoundly more significant for the achievers themselves. Having endured every trial and navigated every challenge, they alone fully understand and cherish the profound joy and satisfaction of that ultimate moment of success.

The Joy of the Journey

There is a unique joy in discovering and living your dream. Imagine working for the sheer pleasure of it, waking up excited every day, loving what you do to the point where a long vacation sounds dull—that is the essence of truly living.

When you realise your dream, the rewards are immensely fulfilling, and rightly so for anyone who achieves their dreams. This success breeds excitement and enthusiasm, fuelling your desire to build on this success and push your dream even further, armed with the knowledge that you possess the qualities and abilities to achieve anything you envision.

However, the realisation of your dream is not the endpoint of your journey. There is one more crucial step to undertake, one that transforms an ordinary individual into a Hero.

Fulfilled Life

Joseph Campbell once said, "When we quit thinking primarily about ourselves and our own self-preservation, we undergo a truly heroic transformation of consciousness."

This transformation is pivotal in the Hero's Journey. It represents the final step where you not only achieve your dreams but also become a true Hero. The journey includes two critical moments of resistance: the initial refusal to accept the call to adventure - and a lesser-known resistance - the refusal of the return. This occurs when Heroes, having obtained their reward, find themselves so content that they do not wish to leave their blissful state.

Yet, the journey only completes when you bring the "elixir of life" back to your community and share it with others. The path of a Hero is not one of selfishness; it is about making life meaningful beyond personal gain.

Peter Burwash articulates this beautifully, noting that while our bodies have physical limits, our capacity to serve others is boundless. He observes, "People who are the happiest in the world are those who are doing things for others."

This service to others not only completes the Hero's Journey but also fulfils a deeper, more altruistic purpose in life.

Journey Completed

"If something you do helps just one person, you've done something wonderful."

~ Blake Mycoskie

This sentiment captures the essence of the final step in the Hero's Journey: giving back. The act of helping others, regardless of the scale, brings a lasting joy that might make you question whether the true purpose of pursuing your dream was to reach this point, where a vision greater than yourself becomes your driving force.

Regardless of where you are on your journey, or even if you have not started yet, you can begin to give back now. However, there is an essential guideline to follow which ensures that your help is truly empowering and not disempowering. Avoid doing for others what they can do for themselves, as this can lead to dependence rather than empowerment. Instead, focus on inspiring and encouraging them, helping instil belief in their capabilities, and providing opportunities that enable them to improve their circumstances.

This approach not only aids them at the moment but empowers them to take charge of their lives. Ultimately, empowering others to fulfil their own destinies is perhaps the most profound act anyone can undertake on their journey.

The Hero in You

Completing the final step on the Hero's Journey transforms you into a whole human being - a true Hero. This transformation extends beyond your initial limits, enhancing your mind and consciousness. You gain a clear understanding that life operates in precise and understandable ways, influenced by the compassion you develop for others. As your compassion grows, it dissolves confusion, suffering, and fear, replacing them with higher intelligence and knowing that surpasses what can be learned from books and formal education.

You begin to see all of humanity as one family, experiencing profound peace and an absolute joy for life. This narrative of unity and discovery is not just your story; it is your destiny. Every step you take, every accomplishment you strive for, and every dream you pursue is in search of eternal happiness. This quest continues relentlessly, up every hill and down every dale, until you ultimately realise that the eternal happiness you seek resides in discovering your true self.

This realisation marks the completion of the Hero's Journey for everyone on planet Earth. The truth of who you really are can only be discovered by you. Until then, the Hero within you persists, calling out day after day, throughout the ages.

PART IV

THE SUMMIT OF ACHIEVEMENT

Joseph Campbell, an influential American scholar and mythologist, deeply explored the psychological underpinnings of myths across various cultures. His seminal work, "The Hero with a Thousand Faces" (1949), introduced the Hero's Journey - a universal motif of adventure and transformation that he termed the monomyth. This concept gained broader recognition through Campbell's engaging dialogue in "The Power of Myth," televised interviews with Bill Moyers broadcast on PBS in 1988.

The Hero's Journey resonates across all human cultures and has been a template for countless stories and religious narratives. It reflects a profound narrative arc that anyone can apply within their personal and professional life. For instance, an entrepreneur might leave a stable job to start a new venture, or a CEO may step down to seek a more fulfilling path, illustrating the initial "call to adventure" that Campbell describes. I experienced this call in 2006 when I transitioned from a banking career to establishing a wellness and coaching practice.

Many ignore this call due to fear, perceived obligations, or comfort with the status quo, leading to a life of unfulfilled potential and regret. However, those who embrace the call often encounter mentors and unexpected allies - modern-day equivalents of Campbell's protective figures who provide "amulets" against forthcoming challenges.

As the journey progresses, individuals confront "threshold guardians" – forces that test their resolve and capacity to venture into the unknown. These guardians symbolise the boundaries of one's current capabilities and the fears of stepping into new, uncharted territories. This stage is not just about overcoming external challenges but also about wrestling with internal conflicts and self-doubt, which Campbell argues are essential aspects of the journey.

Leaders who navigate these trials successfully often find that their journey does not end with one victory; it merely leads to further challenges and responsibilities. They must learn to integrate their achievements into their broader community or organisation - a process Campbell equates to the return of the Hero with a boon for society.

Ultimately, Campbell's monomyth is not just a story structure but a metaphor for personal growth and leadership. It teaches that the path to greatness involves continuous self-awareness, learning, and an unyielding commitment to navigating the complex interplay between external challenges and internal growth. The Hero's Journey thus offers not just a roadmap for achieving success but also a deeper understanding of human resilience and transformation. This narrative empowers us to view our individual pursuits not merely as quests for personal achievement but as contributions to a larger story of community and societal renewal.

This highlights not only the sense of endless struggle that leaders often experience but also the realisation that the skills and capabilities that have helped them succeed to date are insufficient to allow them to overcome the "succession of trials" they now face. Success in these new realms will require a commitment to growth and a willingness to learn.

As Campbell so aptly reminds us, success is seldom achieved without significant challenges. The initial foray into the realm of trials is merely the commencement of a long and arduous journey filled with perilous obstacles and enlightening moments. Heroes must continuously confront formidable dragons and overcome unexpected barriers, encountering numerous transient victories and ephemeral joys along the way.

The intensity of these struggles can be disheartening and exhausting, yet such emotional turmoil is not entirely negative. The leadership journey is akin to an emotional rollercoaster that can plunge individuals into despair but also lift them to exhilarating heights, offering brief glimpses of what might be achieved. These peak experiences, while taxing, are essential for developing the resilience needed to sustainably manage these extremes through emotional regulation and self-care.

However, the most significant battles are often internal. Campbell does not deny the reality of external adversaries; indeed, there are many dragons to slay and barriers to conquer. Yet, he emphasises the crucial role of self-awareness in these struggles. Leaders frequently overlook their less desirable traits - the underlying "carnivorous, lecherous fever" that drives many personal and professional ambitions. This oversight leaves them vulnerable to fears, anxieties, and unchecked desires. The most effective leaders are those who can confront their imperfections openly and responsibly, without defensiveness or blame.

Upon overcoming these external and internal challenges, the Hero recognises the continuing journey ahead. After the quest is achieved, the Hero must return with their transformative trophy. This cycle, central to the monomyth, demands that the Hero reintegrate their newfound wisdom back into society, where it can rejuvenate their community.

This process underscores that no victory is definitive, and a leader's work is perpetually ongoing. Achieving a goal is a cause for celebration, yet it also marks the beginning of new responsibilities - to utilise the gained boon effectively.

Surprisingly, achieving a significant milestone often marks the start of a new chapter rather than its conclusion. This is a fundamental challenge of success: determining the next steps after a victory. Leaders may anticipate a simpler life post-achievement, but they often face new complexities, especially as their success can alter relationships, increasing social distance.

These challenges can manifest in various ways: a founder may see that initial supporters struggle to adapt to a scaled venture; a mid-stage leader might find relationships with early employees becoming more formal and less rewarding; a CEO who sells their company must navigate the new dynamics of the acquiring entity.

Despite these hurdles, the leader's ultimate role is to bridge and integrate these realms, embodying the essence of the entire journey. Upon returning from the dark unknown where adventures were had, the leader must transition from Hero to humble steward, integrating the lessons of the mythic journey into everyday life.

This adjustment is crucial, as failure to do so can alienate the leader from their community and exact a personal toll. Leaders who remain fixated on seeking greater achievements without grounding themselves risk continued strife and dissatisfaction.

The Bhagavad Gita advises detachment from the outcomes of actions, urging leaders to engage in their duties without attachment to results, thus promoting a serene engagement with life's challenges. "Do without attachment the work you have to do... Surrendering all action to Me, with mind intent on the Self, freeing yourself from longing and selfishness, fight - unperturbed by grief." (Bhagavad Gita, 3:19 and 3:30).

This philosophy encourages embracing the Hero's Journey, focusing on the journey itself rather than its endpoints, and finding fulfilment in the ongoing process rather than fleeting achievements.

Through the synthesis of thoughts from profound thinkers like Carl Jung, Pablo Picasso, James Joyce, and Sinclair Lewis, and the wisdom of ancient texts like the Bhagavad Gita, the Bible, Greek mythology, and the Tibetan Book of the Dead, Campbell crafted a timeless framework that connects modern consciousness with eternal truths, guiding individuals on their own journeys from mediocrity to greatness.

PART V

TRANSFORMATION AND EXPLORATION OF THE HERO'S JOURNEY (THE EVOLUTION OF A TIMELESS FRAMEWORK)

From ancient myths to modern cinema, the Hero's Journey remains a powerful framework that speaks to the universal quest for growth and self-discovery. This guide delves into each stage of the Hero's Journey, originally laid out by Christopher Vogler, providing an enriched understanding and practical tips for using it to create unforgettable stories. As we navigate through these twelve steps, we will reference popular movies and literature, such as "The Hobbit," "Harry Potter," "The Lord of the Rings," and "Jack and the Beanstalk," to illustrate the transformative power of the Hero's Journey.

The Hero's Journey is a narrative structure that has evolved over time, influenced by various scholars and storytellers. This chapter explores its development:

- Joseph Campbell's Monomyth: The foundation of the Hero's Journey with 17 stages in "The Hero with a Thousand Faces."

- David Adams Leeming and Phil Cousineau's Interpretations: An adaptation with 8 stages.

- Christopher Vogler's 12-Step Model: The modern, accessible version used by Hollywood writers, including the famous "Star Wars" saga by George Lucas.

The Core Structure of the Hero's Journey

The Hero's Journey is divided into three distinct acts, each marking a critical phase of transformation:

1. **Departure (The Call Beyond the Known):** The Hero leaves behind their ordinary world and steps into the unknown.

2. **Initiation (Trials of the Unknown):** The Hero faces trials, gains allies, and undergoes profound personal growth.

3. **Return (The Hero's Revelation):** The Hero returns to their ordinary world, transformed and bearing newfound wisdom.

Act I – The Departure

1. The Ordinary World: A Life of Predictable Comfort

The journey begins in the Hero's ordinary world, where life is safe but unremarkable. The Hero lives in a peaceful haven, but evil strikes from within or without. The mundane nature of this existence emphasises the dramatic contrast between the familiar and the extraordinary. We may see evidence of a fatal flaw in the Hero at this early point in the story.

It starts with relatable, everyday settings to ground the audience before pulling them into the extraordinary.

Example: Harry Potter's life with the Dursleys is one of routine and neglect, setting the stage for his discovery of the magical world.

2. The Call to Adventure: An Invitation to Greatness

The Hero receives a call to leave their ordinary world and embark on a transformative journey. This could be in the form of an invitation, a challenge, or a life-altering event. This call might manifest as a career change, a new business venture, or a shift towards a life more aligned with one's true passions.

Many people experience this call, yet often resist due to fear, responsibilities, or disbelief in their ability to change their lives significantly. This resistance, while common, can lead to a life of regret or eventual acceptance and transformation if the call is later embraced.

It is a moment of intrigue or danger to capture the audience's attention and signal the beginning of the adventure. The Hero must make a choice about whether to undertake the adventure.

Example: Jack is offered magic beans in exchange for a cow, sparking his adventure up the beanstalk.

3. Refusal of the Call: The Fear of the Unknown

Initially, the Hero refuses the call due to fear, self-doubt, or a desire for safety. This hesitation highlights the Hero's humanity and vulnerability.

As is true of everyone, the Hero hesitates or bumbles at the call and reveals his or her weakness or mortality. The Hero attempts to refuse the adventure because of fear.

The refusal creates tension, emphasising the stakes and making the eventual acceptance more impactful. They may feel unprepared or inadequate or may not want to sacrifice what is being asked of them.

Example: Odysseus pretends to be insane to avoid going to war in "The Odyssey."

4. Meeting the Mentor: Guidance from the Wise

Upon accepting the call, the Hero encounters a mentor or protective figure who provides guidance and tools to face forthcoming challenges. The mentor provides essential guidance, support, and sometimes magical tools to prepare the Hero for the journey ahead.

These figures may not always be as mystical as those in myths, but their role is crucial. They symbolise destiny's protective power, appearing when the Hero shows readiness for transformation.

In real life, these mentors could be a sudden contact offering an unexpected opportunity, or a long-forgotten acquaintance who emerges with crucial advice or assistance.

The mentor often embodies wisdom and experience, setting the Hero up for success and encouraging readers to seek mentors in their own lives.

Example: Gandalf guides Bilbo in "The Hobbit," providing both wisdom and practical tools.

5. Crossing the First Threshold: Entering the Unknown

The next phase involves crossing the threshold from the known world into the realm of adventure and challenge, where threshold guardians appear. The Hero crosses a point of no return, entering the realm of adventure where the rules and challenges are entirely different from their ordinary world.

These guardians represent the Hero's current limitations and the fear of the unknown. Overcoming or bypassing these guardians signifies the Hero's readiness to face the unknown and cross a barrier into the new world, likely facing a new threat, obstacle, or danger.

In the business context, this could mean overcoming initial rejections, financial hurdles, or the daunting prospect of scaling a venture.

This step may seem almost inevitable, but a choice the Hero is making. It is a door through which the Hero must pass for the story to really begin.

Example: Katniss volunteers for the Hunger Games, entering a deadly arena where her survival skills are tested.

Act II – The Initiation

6. Trials, Allies, and Enemies: The Tests of Loyalty and Courage

As the journey progresses, the Hero faces trials or tasks, learning lessons and acquiring skills (often through failure). They meet new people and build alliances (possibly through betrayal), and they encounter new enemies, some loyal to the shadow, some only to themselves, and others more chaotic.

These challenges are not just external but also internal, reflecting Campbell's idea that the greatest battles are often against one's inner doubts and fears.

Leaders must navigate through complex situations, making decisions that not only shape their ventures but also their personal growth and self-awareness.

The Hero learns the rules of their new world. They endure tests of strength and tests of will, meet friends, and come face to face with foes. This stage is to build character development and deepen relationships among characters.

Example: Frodo and his companions face treacherous landscapes, battles, and betrayal in "The Lord of the Rings."

7. The Approach to the Innermost Cave: Facing the True Challenge

The Hero prepares for a significant challenge, often facing their deepest fears or the story's central conflict.

The Hero pauses before finally confronting the Shadow. A loyal retainer may betray or abandon the Hero here. Setbacks occur, sometimes causing the Hero to try a new approach or adopt new ideas.

This is a lesson in persistence for the Hero. When they fail, they need to try again. This stage creates tension and anticipation, preparing the audience for the climax.

Example: Jack confronts the giant in "Jack and the Beanstalk."

8. The Ordeal: The Ultimate Test of Survival

The Hero faces their most significant challenge, often a life-or-death battle or a profound psychological crisis. The Hero attempts to defeat the shadow by confronting them and their stronghold or guardians.

This is the make-or-break moment, emphasising the Hero's growth and resilience. This will be something the Hero barely manages to accomplish.

Example: In "Land of the Living," Abbie faces her kidnapper in a deadly confrontation.

9. Apotheosis and The Ultimate Boon: The Reward and Transformation

The climax of the journey is the Hero's apotheosis, where significant transformation occurs, followed by the achievement of the ultimate boon – whether it is a successful business, personal enlightenment, or another form of success.

After surviving near-death, the Hero earns a reward or accomplishes the goal. A false prize is granted to the Hero, usually a weapon, wealth, wisdom, or mate. This reward does not meet the Hero's internal needs.

The Hero is a changed person now, though he may not fully realise the extent of the change in the continued focus on the matter at hand.

However, this success is not the end but a point of transition, emphasising that every end is a new beginning.

Example: Jack acquires the giant's harp and golden eggs.

Act III – The Return

10. The Road Back: The Journey Home with Wisdom

The Hero attempts to defeat the shadow by confronting them and their stronghold or guardians.

The Hero experiences a major hurdle or obstacle, such as a life-or-death crisis. He comes face to face with his weaknesses and must overcome them.

This will be something the Hero barely manages to accomplish. It emphasises the importance of persistence and reflection on the journey back.

Example: Abby returns in the movie "Harvest," seeking justice.

11. The Hero Rising from the Dead (Resurrection): The Final Battle

The Hero faces one last test, representing a final confrontation that often requires a significant sacrifice. This final test is where everything is at stake, and they must use everything they have learned.

The shadow kills the Hero or their dreams, but the Hero is resurrected due to their strength, cleverness, ingenuity, or purity. This moment underscores the Hero's ultimate transformation and readiness for their new role.

Example: Jason's confrontation in "Dark Matter" symbolises death and rebirth.

12. The Return with the Elixir: Sharing the Hard-Won Wisdom

Finally, the Hero must return to the ordinary world with the wisdom or gift gained from the adventure that can benefit their community; with the blessings of victory, usually including peace, hope, or faith, in addition to other rewards.

This stage highlights the Hero's impact on the world and the power of transformation.

The true mark of a Hero lies in their ability to use their achievements to rejuvenate and renew their community or field. The Hero brings their knowledge or the "elixir" back to the ordinary world, where they apply it to help all who remain there. This phase involves reconciling the extraordinary experiences of the journey with everyday reality.

Example: Harry returns to Hogwarts with the Philosopher's Stone, symbolising the triumph of good over evil.

PART VI

A COMPREHENSIVE GUIDE TO POWERFUL STORYTELLING

The Hero's Journey is a timeless narrative structure that captivates readers, allowing them to resonate deeply with characters who face trials, grow, and ultimately transform. This chapter offers beginner-friendly tips and practical techniques to leverage the Hero's Journey in crafting compelling stories. It balances the classic framework with creativity, ensuring your unique voice shines through.

This comprehensive and detailed script provides an enriched approach to using the Hero's Journey, combining actionable tips, and creative insights to help storytellers, marketers, and creators make the most of this powerful narrative framework.

Embracing Structure with Flexibility - The Art of Balancing Structure and Creativity

While the Hero's Journey provides a solid framework for storytelling, it is crucial to remain flexible and allow creative twists to emerge. Understand each stage of the journey, but do not feel confined to a rigid checklist.

If your protagonist is ready for the adventure without fear, skip the "Refusal of the Call." If there is no mentor, let the protagonist find their way alone. The journey must serve the story, not the other way around.

Crafting a Gripping Beginning - an Engaging Call to Adventure

Start with an intriguing event or mystery that captures both the protagonist's and the reader's attention. This event should ignite a strong emotional connection and set the stakes high.

Establish why the adventure matters to your protagonist. What do they stand to gain or lose? What are their dreams, ambitions, or fears that propel them into the unknown?

Present Conflict or Disruption in the Ordinary World

Create a situation where the protagonist must face a choice, propelling them out of their comfort zone.

Show the potential growth or consequences of inaction to make the stakes clear. This will create a powerful drive for the protagonist to embark on their journey.

Developing Relatable and Compelling Heroes with Depth

A great Hero is multi-dimensional, with both flaws and desires that drive their journey. If they are already perfect, there is no room for growth, no conflict to overcome, and no story to tell.

Give your Heroes desires that motivate them and flaws that make them human. They should have something they long for and something that holds them back.

Ensure Flaws Fit with the Challenges Ahead

Make sure your Hero's flaws align with the challenges they will face. This creates a coherent narrative where their growth is both believable and satisfying.

If a Hero's flaw is fear, then their journey should force them to face situations that push them beyond their comfort zone.

Designing Memorable Supporting Characters – the Allies and Adversaries

The story is not just about the Hero; the supporting characters - both allies and adversaries - are essential in shaping the journey. Make them memorable and believable with distinct traits and motivations.

Each character should have their own values, fears, and desires, which affect their interactions with the Hero. This will create a dynamic narrative full of tension and unexpected turns.

Create Interesting Dynamics and Conflicts

Allies and adversaries should not just be flat characters; their beliefs, goals, and personalities should either complement or clash with the Hero's, creating rich, dynamic relationships.

Consider unexpected alliances or betrayals, shaped by the characters' backstories and current motivations.

Creating Tension and the Internal and External Conflicts

A compelling narrative balances internal conflicts - moral dilemmas, self-doubt, conflicting emotions - with external conflicts like opposing forces or challenging events.

Internal conflicts add depth to the character, while external conflicts drive the plot forward, creating a captivating narrative rhythm.

Alternate Between Fast-Paced and Reflective Moments

A dynamic story needs variation in pacing. Alternate between action-packed sequences and quieter, introspective moments to build tension and anticipation.

This balance keeps readers engaged, providing them with breathers between intense scenes while also deepening emotional connections.

Showcasing Hero's Transformational Growth Through Ordeals

The journey's ordeals should push the Hero to their limits, forcing them to confront their fears, make tough decisions, or face their past.

The ordeal must be significant, serving as a turning point that catalyses both internal and external transformations.

Explore Emotional Impact and Vulnerability

Showcase how the Hero's ordeals affect them emotionally. Delve into their reactions, doubts, and moments of vulnerability to allow readers to connect deeply with their experiences.

Allow the reader to see the Hero's internal changes – beliefs, mindset, values – alongside their external actions.

Crafting Satisfying Resolutions with Meaningful Closure

Ensure all major plot points are resolved to avoid leaving readers feeling unsatisfied. Characters should achieve personal growth, completing their arcs in a way that resonates with the reader.

Closure does not mean every story ends happily, but every story should feel complete. Show how the Hero has changed and what they have learned.

THE CYCLICAL JOURNEY OR QUEST UNDERTAKEN BY ANY HERO

(A UNIVERSAL PATHWAY IN STORIES AND LIFE)

The Hero's Journey is a timeless narrative structure that resonates across genres - science fiction, fantasy, adventure, thriller, and even real-life experiences. At its core, it is about transformation - leaving the comfort of the known, facing challenges in the unknown, and returning as a changed person.

While the Hero's Journey is often associated with genres like fantasy and adventure, its fundamental principles of transformation, conflict, and growth can be applied to almost any story where a protagonist is drawn from their ordinary world into a series of life-altering conflicts.

This chapter introduces a few compelling examples from literature - a psychological thriller and a supernatural novel - to demonstrate the adaptability of the Hero's Journey framework. They are **Dean Koontz's "Intensity"** and **Stephen King's "The Dead Zone."**

Narrated thereafter are five feature films in which the protagonist is drawn out of their ordinary life into a series of challenging conflicts that physically and/or emotionally transform them. These are: **Star Wars (1977), The Matrix (1999), Slumdog Millionaire (2008), Avatar (2009), and Aladdin (2019).**

Each example is mapped to the Hero's Journey's twelve steps, showcasing how versatile and impactful this framework can be.

Example 1: The Relentless Pursuit in "Intensity" by Dean Koontz

"Intensity" is a psychological thriller that takes the reader on a gripping 24-hour journey of survival, courage, and transformation. Chyna Shepard, the protagonist, confronts her fears and the horrors of a serial killer to save herself and another victim.

Here is how her story unfolds through the lens of the Hero's Journey:

1. The Ordinary World: A Fragile Sanctuary

Chyna Shepard accompanies her best friend, Laura, to her childhood home for a peaceful weekend. Both are psychology students, and Chyna, still scarred by her abusive past, hopes for some respite.

2. The Call to Adventure: A Night of Terror

Their plans for relaxation are shattered when a ruthless serial killer, Edgler Vess, invades the home and kills Laura's family. Chyna hears Laura's cries for help, igniting a sense of responsibility and a call to action.

3. Refusal of the Call: Overwhelmed by Fear

Chyna, terrified and weaponless, hides while Vess takes Laura away. Her fear and sense of inadequacy almost paralyse her into inaction.

4. Meeting the Mentor: A Voice of Conscience

Chyna's mentor takes the form of her inner conscience - memories of her own suffering and Laura's selfless friendship compel her to act. She cannot let another person suffer as she once did.

5. Crossing the First Threshold: Entering the Predator's Lair

Driven by guilt and determination, Chyna sneaks into Vess's motorhome, hiding in the darkness as he drives off.

6. **Tests, Allies, and Enemies: Survival Against the Odds**

After discovering Laura is already dead, Chyna decides to save Vess's next victim, a 16-year-old girl named Ariel. Her primary allies are her fierce will to survive and her empathy for other victims, while her enemies are Vess and her own lack of preparation.

7. Approach to the Inmost Cave: Stepping into the Lion's Den

Chyna follows Vess to his secluded home, stealthily entering the house in search of Ariel.

8. The Ordeal: A Struggle for Freedom

Vess discovers Chyna, captures her, and ties her up. She sinks into despair, questioning whether she has any chance of survival.

9. The Reward: A Glimmer of Hope

Chyna finds hope in an unexpected sight - an elk calmly moving among the killers' vicious guard dogs. This improbable scenario renews her determination to escape.

10. The Road Back: Fleeing with the Innocent

After a harrowing escape involving shattered furniture and injury, Chyna rescues Ariel and escapes into the motorhome.

11. The Resurrection: A Fiery Confrontation

Vess catches up, shooting at the motorhome and causing a crash. Chyna sets him on fire and narrowly escapes the flames.

12. The Return with the Elixir: A New Beginning

Chyna decides to change her field of study from psychology to literature, adopting Ariel and helping her recover from her trauma.

Example 2: The Psychic's Struggle in "The Dead Zone" by Stephen King

"The Dead Zone" tells the story of Johnny Smith, a man who awakens from a coma with psychic abilities that change his life forever. Through his journey, he grapples with his newfound power, the responsibility it brings, and the moral dilemmas that follow.

Hero's Journey Breakdown:

1. The Ordinary World: A Simple Life Shattered.

Johnny Smith is a teacher who lives a simple life with his girlfriend, Sarah. One night turns tragic when a taxi ride home from the county fair results in a devastating accident that leaves him in a coma for 55 months.

2. The Call to Adventure: Awakening to New Powers

Johnny awakens from his coma with the ability to see glimpses of the past, present, and future of people he touches. He begins to use this power, albeit reluctantly, to help others.

3. Refusal of the Call: The Burden of Unwanted Power

Johnny does not want to use his psychic abilities as it isolates him and makes him a curiosity among people.

4. Meeting the Mentor: Encouragement from Belief

Johnny's doctor and father believe in his abilities and encourage him to use them for good, driving him to help solve a murder case.

5. Crossing the First Threshold: Embracing His Role

Johnny decides to collaborate with the police to solve a series of murders, taking his first step towards embracing his psychic role.

6. Tests, Allies, and Enemies: Navigating a Treacherous Path

Over time, Johnny's abilities are tested without significant publicity. His main allies include his father, doctor, and Sarah. His chief adversary becomes Greg Stillson, a ruthless political candidate.

7. Approach to the Inmost Cave: The Terrifying Vision

Johnny touches Stillson and sees a future where he starts a world war, causing untold destruction. He realises the gravity of his gift but knows no one will believe him.

8. The Ordeal: Prophecy of Disaster

Despite predicting a fire that kills many children, Johnny's warnings go unheeded, teaching him that his powers are both a gift and a curse.

9. The Reward: The Clarity of Conviction

This tragedy solidifies Johnny's belief in his psychic abilities, but it also makes him realise the futility of trying to convince others before disaster strikes.

10. The Road Back: A Quiet Determination

Johnny takes various low-profile jobs while still tracking Stillson's activities, preparing for what he knows must be done.

11. The Resurrection: The Final Decision

Realising he is dying and has limited time, Johnny decides to assassinate Stillson. Although he fails, he exposes Stillson's true nature when he uses a child as a shield.

12. The Return with the Elixir: A Hero's Final Peace

Johnny dies in peace, knowing he has saved the world from a catastrophic future, accepting his fate with serenity.

Example 3: A Galactic Awakening in "Star Wars (1977)" by George Lucas

"Star Wars: A New Hope" is a space opera that chronicles Luke Skywalker's journey from a humble farm boy to a key figure in the Rebel Alliance's fight against the tyrannical Galactic Empire. Through his quest, Luke learns the ways of the Force, confronts his fears, and embraces his destiny as a Jedi Knight, becoming a beacon of hope for a galaxy in turmoil.

Hero's Journey Breakdown:

1. The Ordinary World: A Desert Dreamer

Luke Skywalker lives on the desert planet Tatooine with his aunt and uncle, leading a mundane life as a farm boy.

2. Call to Adventure: A Princess's Plea

Luke stumbles upon a message from Princess Leia hidden in R2-D2, calling for help against the Empire.

3. Refusal of the Call: Bound by Duty

Luke initially hesitates, feeling tied to his family's responsibilities and unsure of venturing into the unknown.

4. Meeting with the Mentor: The Wisdom of the Jedi

Luke meets Obi-Wan Kenobi, who introduces him to the ways of the Force and the history of the Jedi.

5. Crossing the Threshold: Into the Stars

After his aunt and uncle are killed by the Empire's stormtroopers, Luke decides to leave Tatooine and join the Rebel Alliance.

6. Tests, Allies, and Enemies: Rebels and Rogues

Luke teams up with Han Solo, Chewbacca, and Princess Leia. They face several challenges, including escaping the Death Star and confronting Darth Vader's forces.

7. Approach to the Inmost Cave: A Desperate Plan

Luke and his allies discover the Death Star plans, realising the massive threat it poses. They prepare for the final assault.

8. The Ordeal: The Battle of Yavin

The Rebel Alliance launches an attack on the Death Star. Luke must trust in the Force to guide him during the high-stakes battle.

9. The Reward: A Galaxy's Hope

Luke successfully destroys the Death Star, dealing a significant blow to the Empire.

10. The Road Back: The Escape from Darkness

Luke and his companions return to the Rebel base, having achieved a major victory.

11. The Resurrection: The Birth of a Hero

The celebration is bittersweet, with the looming presence of the Empire's remaining forces. Luke is now seen as a rising Hero of the Rebellion.

12. The Return with the Elixir: A New Dawn

Luke has gained newfound confidence, purpose, and mastery of the Force, setting the stage for his continued journey as a Jedi.

Example 4: The Hacker's Redemption in "The Matrix (1999)" by Lana and Lily Wachowski

"The Matrix" is a mind-bending sci-fi thriller that follows Neo, a computer hacker who uncovers a shocking truth about reality. Guided by Morpheus and a group of rebels, Neo is thrust into a battle against the machine-controlled simulation, forcing him to embrace his role as "The One." His journey from doubt to self-realisation transforms him into the saviour humanity desperately needs.

Hero's Journey Breakdown:

The Ordinary World: A Digital Prison

Neo lives a double life as Thomas Anderson, a software programmer by day and a hacker by night.

Call to Adventure: The Truth Revealed

Neo receives cryptic messages from the hacker Morpheus, who offers him the chance to learn the truth about "The Matrix."

Refusal of the Call: The Chains of Fear

Neo hesitates, doubting the reality of the Matrix and fearing the consequences of accepting the truth.

Meeting with the Mentor: Choosing the Red Pill

Neo meets Morpheus, who explains the Matrix's illusion and offers him a choice between the red pill (truth) and the blue pill (ignorance).

Crossing the Threshold: Awakening to Reality

Neo takes the red pill and awakens in the real world, where he learns that humans are enslaved by machines.

Tests, Allies, and Enemies: Battles Within and Without

Neo undergoes training to manipulate the Matrix and learns to fight against its sentient programmes, especially the agents led by Agent Smith.

Approach to the Inmost Cave: A Mission to Save Morpheus

Neo must rescue Morpheus, who has been captured and tortured by the agents.

The Ordeal: The Duel with the Agent

Neo faces a showdown with Agent Smith, confronting his fear of death and the reality of his role as "The One."

The Reward: Becoming "The One"

Neo realises his powers within the Matrix, mastering control over its code and defeating Agent Smith.

The Road Back: Fighting for Liberation

Neo begins to believe in his destiny as "The One" and commits to liberating more minds from the Matrix.

The Resurrection: The Power to Change Reality

Neo is seemingly killed by Agent Smith but resurrects with newfound abilities, confirming his role as the saviour.

The Return with the Elixir: A Promise of Freedom

Neo, now empowered and fully awakened, vows to end the Matrix's control over humanity.

Example 5: A Destiny Written in Poverty in "Slumdog Millionaire (2008)" by Vikas Swarup

"Slumdog Millionaire" is a riveting drama that tells the story of Jamal Malik, a young man from the slums of Mumbai whose life is transformed when he becomes a contestant on "Who Wants to Be a Millionaire?" As he answers each question, flashbacks reveal his troubled past, revealing how fate, love, and resilience have prepared him to win both the game and his lost love.

Hero's Journey Breakdown:

The Ordinary World: A Life of Survival

Jamal lives in the slums of Mumbai, working as a "Chaiwala" (tea server) in a call centre.

Call to Adventure: A Chance for Change

Jamal participates in "Who Wants to Be a Millionaire?" with the hope that Latika, his lost love, might see him on TV.

Refusal of the Call: The Weight of Scepticism

Though he participates, Jamal is unsure if he is making the right choice, knowing the risks and disbelief surrounding his success.

Meeting with the Mentor: Life as a Teacher

Jamal has no traditional mentor but relies on his life experiences, which guide him through the answers on the show.

Crossing the Threshold: Stepping into the Spotlight

Jamal starts winning each round of the game, using his past experiences to answer the questions correctly.

Tests, Allies, and Enemies: Battles with Fate

He faces various challenges, including the host's scepticism, the police's brutal interrogation, and the threat of gangsters.

Approach to the Inmost Cave: The Final Question

Jamal reaches the final question, facing the ultimate test of knowledge and faith.

The Ordeal: The Leap of Faith

Jamal makes a guess on the final question without knowing the answer, trusting his intuition and fate.

The Reward: A Victory Beyond Wealth

Jamal wins the grand prize, becoming a millionaire.

The Road Back: Seeking His Lost Love

As Jamal exits the game show, he is free from suspicion and searches for Latika.

The Resurrection: Love Reclaimed

Jamal finds Latika, who has escaped her captors, and they are reunited.

The Return with the Elixir: A Tale of True Riches

Jamal has won both the money and the love of his life, showing that love and fate are the true rewards.

Example 6: The Warrior's Rebirth in "Avatar (2009)" by James Cameron

"Avatar" is a visually stunning epic that centres on Jake Sully, a paraplegic Marine who embarks on a mission to the alien moon Pandora. Through his avatar, Jake experiences a profound transformation, choosing to protect the indigenous Na'vi people and their sacred land from human exploitation. His journey is one of rediscovery, where he finds purpose, love, and a new identity in an alien world.

Hero's Journey Breakdown:

The Ordinary World: A Warrior's Disillusionment

Jake Sully lives on Earth, disillusioned and in a wheelchair after losing the use of his legs in combat.

Call to Adventure: A Second Chance on Pandora

Jake is offered a chance to travel to Pandora and operate an "avatar" body in exchange for a valuable mission.

Refusal of the Call: Doubt in the Unknown

Jake hesitates, unsure of what he can contribute, feeling out of place among scientists and sceptics.

Meeting with the Mentor: Wisdom of the Na'vi

Neytiri, a Na'vi warrior, becomes Jake's guide, teaching him the ways of her people and the beauty of Pandora.

Crossing the Threshold: Embracing the Na'vi Way

Jake chooses to stay in his avatar form, fully embracing Na'vi culture and rejecting his original mission.

Tests, Allies, and Enemies: Between Two Worlds

Jake forms bonds with the Na'vi, especially Neytiri, but faces hostility from both humans and some Na'vi who distrust him.

Approach to the Inmost Cave: Defending Pandora's Heart

The humans plan to destroy the Na'vi's sacred Tree of Souls. Jake knows he must lead the Na'vi in a battle against his former allies.

The Ordeal: The Battle for Pandora

A climactic battle ensues between the Na'vi and the humans, in which Jake fights for Pandora's survival.

The Reward: Victory for the Na'vi.

Jake helps defeat the human forces and saves the Na'vi, earning his place among them.

The Road Back: A Permanent Choice

With the immediate threat gone, Jake decides to stay permanently in his avatar form.

The Resurrection: Becoming One with Pandora

Jake undergoes a final ritual to transfer his consciousness permanently into his avatar body.

The Return with the Elixir: A Guardian Reborn

Jake becomes one with Pandora, fully integrating into Na'vi life and forever changing the dynamic between humans and the Na'vi.

Example 7: The Street Thief's Transformation in "Aladdin (2019)" by John August and Others

"Aladdin" is a magical adventure that follows the journey of a street-smart young man who stumbles upon a magic lamp containing a powerful genie. As Aladdin uses his wishes to win the love of Princess Jasmine and outwit the wicked sorcerer Jafar, he learns the value of honesty and self-worth, transforming from a mere thief to a true prince in spirit and heart.

Hero's Journey Breakdown:

The Ordinary World: A Life of Scraps

Aladdin lives as a poor street thief in the bustling city of Agrabah, stealing to survive.

Call to Adventure: The Cave of Wonders

Aladdin encounters Princess Jasmine and becomes infatuated. He also hears about a cave filled with treasures and a magical lamp.

Refusal of the Call: The Fear of Being Unworthy

Aladdin is unsure if he is worthy of pursuing Jasmine or of achieving anything more than being a street thief.

Meeting with the Mentor: Genie's Guidance

The Genie of the Lamp becomes Aladdin's guide, offering him three wishes and valuable life lessons.

Crossing the Threshold: The Prince's Disguise

Aladdin uses his first wish to become a prince, entering a new world of wealth, power, and deception.

Tests, Allies, and Enemies: Games of Deception

Aladdin navigates palace politics, wins the heart of Jasmine, but faces challenges from the evil sorcerer Jafar.

Approach to the Inmost Cave: Unmasking the Truth

Aladdin must confront his deceit and reclaim his true self after Jafar exposes him as a fraud.

The Ordeal: The Battle Against Jafar

A final showdown against Jafar, who has taken control of the Genie and threatens to destroy Agrabah.

The Reward: Outwitting the Sorcerer

Aladdin outsmarts Jafar by tricking him into wishing to become a genie, imprisoning him in a lamp.

The Road Back: Choosing Freedom

Aladdin returns to Jasmine, realising the importance of being true to himself rather than relying on wishes.

The Resurrection: A New Self Emerges

Aladdin frees the Genie, choosing love and friendship over power.

The Return with the Elixir: Love and Freedom

Aladdin and Jasmine get married, and Aladdin gains a new life full of honesty, love, and newfound purpose.

PART VIII

MY JOURNEY

Drawing inspiration, tips, and techniques from these examples, create your own version of the Hero's Journey by using the worksheet detailed at the end of this chapter. List a scene or moment (in one sentence) that applies to each of the stages; craft your own compelling story using the Hero's Journey framework, balancing structure with creativity, and ensuring your unique voice shines through.

Watch one (or more) of your favourite movies and list the stages the movie has used (narrated earlier - just before this chapter, are a few of the movies which I am sure must have empowered you).

You may like to refer to my own "Cyclical Journey (Quest undertaken)" with all the three distinct acts of the 12-step Journey, each marking a critical phase of transformation.

Act 1: Departure (The Call Beyond the Known)

1. The Ordinary World: A Life of Duality

I began my journey as a high-achieving university graduate and then a successful banker with a stable career. However, beneath the surface of this seemingly perfect life lay a deep-seated dissatisfaction and a yearning for something more meaningful. The life which I was leading was filled with both prestige and pressure, offering security but lacking true fulfilment.

2. The Call to Adventure: Awakening to Inner Conflict

The stress of the banking job, combined with a passion for intellectual wellness distribution on the side, started to reveal cracks in my life's foundation. Despite the newfound joy I found in helping people through wellness ventures, it clashed with my professional life. A desire to break free from a life that no longer aligned with my values began to stir within me.

3. Refusal of the Call: Fear of the Unknown

Though I sensed the need for a change, the fear of letting go of a secure job after 32 years and the uncertainty of what lay ahead created resistance. The comfort of the known kept me tethered to the familiar, masking the deeper longing for transformation.

4. Meeting the Mentor: Wisdom from the Sales and Wellness Industries

My path crossed with a mentor in the wellness direct sales industry who offered guidance, wisdom, and a new perspective on life and business. This mentor, along with other eminent global personalities, played a pivotal role in showing me a different way of living - one rooted in compassion, empathy, and a holistic understanding of wellness.

5. Crossing the First Threshold: Breaking Away from the Old

The turning point came when an unexpected transfer order served as a catalyst for me to leave my prestigious banking job. Choosing to step away from the stability of a career at its peak, I embraced the unknown, fully dedicating myself to the wellness distribution that had long brought me joy.

6. Tests, Allies, and Enemies: Navigating New Paths

In this new chapter, I faced numerous challenges - learning alternative therapies like Emotional Freedom Techniques (EFT) and Qigong, reading empowering books, and attending seminars. I also encountered both support from my wellness community and scepticism from those who doubted my unconventional path.

7. Approach to the Inmost Cave: Embracing Vulnerability

As I delved deeper into my new life, I began to confront my innermost fears and vulnerabilities. This period marked a profound turning point where I faced the emotional and psychological baggage that had been weighing me down. It was a time of confronting the deepest wounds and embracing them as catalysts for growth.

8. The Ordeal: Facing the Abyss

Choosing to remain in the abyss rather than escape, I committed myself to face my deepest fears and pains. This was not about employing old tactics but about embracing vulnerability and allowing true transformation to occur, acknowledging that the only way out was through.

9. The Reward: A New Understanding of Healing

Through surrendering to the process, I gained a deeper understanding of healing - not just as a physical concept but as a holistic journey that integrates the mental, emotional, and spiritual aspects of being. This realisation empowered me to extend my work beyond wellness distribution to encompass a broader, more profound mission.

10. The Road Back: Reconnecting with Authentic Purpose

Emerging from the depths of my transformation, I experienced a renewed sense of purpose and authenticity. I realised that my deepest wounds were not just scars but sanctuaries for nurturing new beginnings, guiding me to reconnect with my true self and passions.

11. The Resurrection: A Rebirth of Vision

With a reinvigorated spirit, I rediscovered my passion for transformation and people. This period marked a significant shift – one where I began to envision a new life aligned with my evolved values, preparing me for the next chapter of my journey.

12. The Return with the Elixir: Sharing the Wisdom

Armed with newfound clarity, confidence, and insights, I have now authored this book "Epic Journey from Mediocrity to Greatness," conducting seminars and workshops that resonate deeply with others. My journey became a testament to the power of transformation, offering others a path to self-discovery and greatness.

Act 2: Initiation (Trials of the Unknown)

1. The Road of Trials: Learning and Unlearning

In this phase, I had immersed myself in learning alternative therapies, healing methods, and the study of holistic wellness. The trials involved not only learning new skills but also unlearning old habits and beliefs that no longer served me a higher purpose.

2. Allies and Supporters: Building a Tribe

I surrounded myself with mentors, wellness professionals, and a community of like-minded individuals who supported my growth and learning. These allies provided emotional and intellectual support as I navigated the challenges of this new path.

3. Facing the Inner Demons: The Battle Within

Confronting old pains, fears, and limiting beliefs became a crucial aspect of this phase. It was not just a journey of external change but an internal battle to redefine my identity and purpose.

4. Embracing New Teachings: The Path of Wisdom

Through continuous learning, attending seminars, and engaging in self-reflection, I acquired new teachings that reshaped my worldview. This period was marked by integrating knowledge and experiences into a coherent understanding of life's purpose.

5. The Ultimate Boon: A Deep Sense of Clarity

This phase culminated in gaining clarity about my mission and purpose. I realised that true fulfilment came from aligning my work with my values - serving others through wellness, transformation, and education.

6. The Abyss: The Dark Night of the Soul

Despite the newfound clarity, I faced moments of doubt, fatigue, and frustration. The journey required me to dive deep into my psyche, confronting existential questions and fears that challenged my resolve.

7. Revelation and Redemption: The Emergence of the New Self.

Having navigated through the abyss, I emerged with a renewed sense of self – stronger, wiser, and more compassionate. This transformation was not just about changing careers but fundamentally altering my relationship with myself and the world.

8. Atonement with Self: Embracing Wholeness

I learned to accept all parts of myself - the strengths, the flaws, the successes, and the failures. This acceptance allowed me to move forward with greater self-love, wisdom, and balance, embodying the true essence of a leader and mentor.

9. The Call to Share: Becoming a Mentor

Having gained so much from my journey, I felt compelled to share my insights with others. This led me to become a mentor and wellness trainer, guiding others to find their paths and embrace their call to greatness.

10. The Mastery of Two Worlds: Harmonising the Inner and Outer

I learned to navigate both the inner world of emotions and spirituality and the outer world of practical achievements and material success. This harmony allowed me to live a life that was both deeply fulfilling and externally successful.

11. The Freedom to Live: A Life of Service and Authenticity

With nothing left to prove and everything to give, I am committed to a life of service, authenticity, and impact. My work became a reflection of my journey, helping others to transform their lives and reach their fullest potential.

12. The Hero's Revelation: A Legacy of Transformation

My journey culminates in the realisation that every experience, challenge, and insight has prepared me for the present moment. The book, the seminars, and the continued growth are my gifts to the world - an invitation for others to embark on their own epic journeys.

Act 3: Return (The Hero's Revelation)

1. The Return to Share: Inspiring Others to Begin Their Journeys

With my newfound wisdom and clarity, I returned not to the ordinary world but to a higher plane where my mission is to inspire others to embark on their own journeys of transformation.

2. Creating a Legacy: Writing "The Call to Greatness"

Through this book, I have attempted to distil the essence of my journey and the Hero's Journey framework, offering readers a practical guide to transforming their own lives and finding their true callings.

3. Building a Community: Leading Workshops and Seminars

I have attempted to create spaces where people come together to learn, grow, and transform. My seminars and workshops are not just events but transformative experiences that catalyse change.

4. Empowering Others: The Role of a Mentor

As a mentor, I empower others to take charge of their lives, guiding them through their fears, helping them navigate the unknown, and encouraging them to embrace their paths.

5. Facing New Challenges: Evolving with Time

Even after all these years, the journey never truly ends. New challenges and opportunities continue to arise, prompting me to evolve and adapt while staying true to my core values.

6. Embracing Continuous Growth: The Journey Within

I recognise that the journey of transformation is cyclical, and there is always room for growth, learning, and deeper self-discovery. Therefore, I remain committed to this ongoing process of evolution.

7. Cultivating Wisdom: Sharing Hard-Earned Insights

I am committed to sharing my hard-earned wisdom with others, not as a prescriptive formula but as an invitation to explore their unique paths. My story can become a guiding light for those seeking their call to greatness.

8. Creating Impact: Guiding Humanity's Next Evolutionary Step

I believe in the "Go-Giver" concept, contributing to humanity's next step of evolution by promoting personal responsibility, empowerment, and authentic adulthood – the qualities I foster in my community.

9. Reaffirming Purpose: Living with Intention

Every day, I choose to live with purpose, aligning my actions with my vision of a world filled with potential, possibility, and promise. My work serves as a daily affirmation of this purpose.

10. The Hero's Return: Celebrating the Journey

Now, at age 70, I reflect on my life's journey with gratitude, celebrating the highs and lows, the challenges and triumphs, and the continuous growth that has defined my path.

11. A Life Fully Lived: Balancing Fulfilment and Impact

I feel I have achieved a balance of personal fulfilment and meaningful impact, demonstrating that a life well-lived is not about avoiding challenges but embracing them with courage and grace.

12. The Eternal Journey: Inspiring Others to Follow

This narrative structure of mine can serve as a powerful testament to the transformative power of the Hero's Journey. Each step offers a relatable and transformative insight based on my real-life experiences.

As you continue to grow and evolve, you inspire countless others to embark on their own quests for greatness.

PART IX

THE 12-STEP "ACTIVITY WORKSHEET" TO CRAFT YOUR OWN "HERO'S JOURNEY"

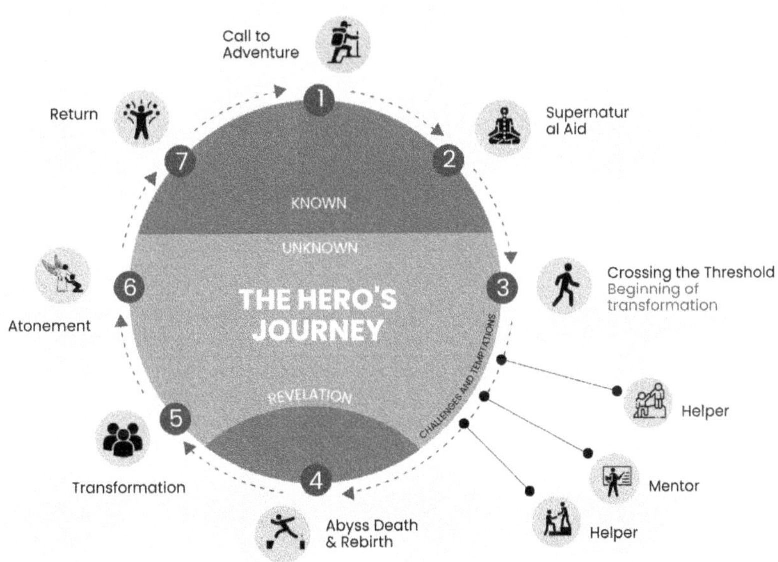

Name: _________________________________   **Date:** ____________

Directions: For any story, answer the questions of each of the steps on the following pages to determine the Hero's Journey.

1. The Ordinary World – What is the Hero's world like at the beginning of the story?

2. Call to Adventure – What happens to prompt the Hero to take a step into the adventure?

3. Refusal of the Call – Does the Hero refuse to go? If so, why?

4. Meeting with the Mentor – Who helps the Hero gain wisdom?

5. Crossing the First Threshold – When does the Hero cross the point of no return in the story?

6. Tests, Allies, and Enemies – How do the other characters affect the Hero?

7. Approach – Does the Hero try and fail? How so? What does he do when he fails?

8. Ordeal – What happens when the story reaches a life-or-death point?

-161-

9. Reward – What does the Hero receive as a reward?

-162-

10. The Road Back – How does the Hero attempt to return to his or her normal life?

11. Resurrection of the Hero – What is the final test?

-164-

12. Return with the Elixir – What knowledge or wisdom does the Hero bring back with him or her?

PART X

EPILOGUE: THE CALL TO GREATNESS

(Transforming Your Life's Journey)

The journey from mediocrity to greatness is akin to the Hero's Journey - a transformative path that leads you back home, changed, and ready to contribute. Your experiences, both triumphs and trials, are not just for you; they are meant to be shared to inspire and elevate others.

This book is not just about changing yourself; it is about changing the world one person at a time, starting with you. Embrace this epic journey and let it guide you to your own greatness.

The Hero's Journey stands as a profound metaphor for the deep, transformative process that unites the narratives of Heroes across all ages and cultures. Through extensive research, Joseph Campbell identified a series of stages common to these Heroes' tales, regardless of their origins. He encapsulated these universal experiences in what he termed the "monomyth."

Joseph Campbell eloquently described it: "A Hero ventures forth from the world of common day into a region of supernatural wonder; fabulous forces are there encountered, and a decisive victory is won. The Hero comes back from this mysterious adventure with the power to bestow boons on his fellow man."

Fundamentally, the Hero's Journey is a sequence of events that catalyses a transformation in the Hero, evolving from their initial state to a profoundly altered new one, often depicted as a "character arc."

This narrative framework is not just a storytelling tool; it reflects a deeper, universal human experience. Reflect on the last film you watched or the book you read; did the protagonist undergo several of these transformative stages? This recurrence is not merely because storytellers consciously employ the Hero's Journey as a narrative formula; it suggests that this pattern is woven into the very fabric of human storytelling, resonating deeply within our collective psyche.

What the Hero's Journey Is Not

Is the Hero's Journey a magical formula for storytelling success? Absolutely not! It is crucial to understand that the Hero's Journey was not concocted by any single individual but emerged as a recurring pattern identified in a multitude of myths and stories across diverse cultures.

"The Hero's Journey was not invented; it was discovered," as noted by Allen Palmer, an Australian screenwriter.

Joseph Campbell explored narratives from every corner of the globe and throughout history, only to find that every culture has been retelling the same fundamental story over and over. The Hero's Journey is not a shortcut to wealth or success; it is a universal narrative framework embedded in the human psyche.

This narrative blueprint existed long before Campbell articulated it, serving as an underlying structure for storytelling across civilisations. Its identification has since provided a valuable toolkit for writers and storytellers, helping them craft stories that resonate deeply and maintain emotional impact.

However, it is important to distinguish that while the Hero's Journey reflects a universal human resonance with transformation and adventure, it does not prescribe specific themes for stories. Utilising the Hero's Journey in writing is not a guarantee of thematic depth or emotional power. These elements depend on the writer's ability to weave complex themes into the fabric of their narrative, which revolves around the central axis of the plot and character development.

Your Challenge

Your life's work should not just be about achieving success; it should resonate with your personal journey that helps you articulate and commit to a mission that not only fulfils you but also contributes to the world.

I invite you to apply the Hero's Journey to develop your protagonist's character arc. Select any number of stages from this framework to shape your character's journey. After doing so, reflect on the experience. Did this method aid in fleshing out your character's arc? Did you find it to be a helpful tool, or did it feel restrictive or overly formulaic? Consider whether embedding a character arc within your story enhances its emotional depth and broad appeal. Would you employ this method again, or do you have other techniques you prefer for character development?

Start to critically observe the stories that you encounter daily. Are you able to spot the stages of the Hero's Journey within them? Reflect on whether this framework affects the story's quality, or if other elements like theme, concept, characterisation, plot, conflict, and tension play more significant roles.

By actively analysing stories, you will enhance your understanding of how various storytelling components interconnect. This practice will improve your ability to harness effective storytelling techniques in your own work. Remember, the Hero's Journey is merely one tool among many in the narrative toolbox, and there is much to explore and understand!

Reading this book (or attending the related seminar) is not merely an academic exercise; it connects the epic narratives of both historical and contemporary myths to our daily lives, framing our personal challenges within a grand, heroic context.

Remember, anyone can become a Hero, whether by intention or accident. However, embracing this path often requires a painful evolution, a prerequisite for achieving greatness. The personal challenges we face can be daunting, tempting us to retreat to comfort rather than confront our fears.

It is hoped that this exploration of classical narratives has empowered you to live a more heroic life, drawing strength from the timeless tales of Heroes, past and present.

Author Bio

Dr. DEBI PRASAD ACHARJYA

(Unlock Potentials – Expand Possibilities)

Dr. Debi Prasad Acharjya is a Wellness Coach, Hydration Specialist, Author, and Functional Nutritionist dedicated to transforming lives through holistic health and personal development.

With a foundation built on academic excellence, including a B.Sc. (Gold Medallist) from St. Aloysius College and a Post Graduate Diploma in Systems Management, his journey has been marked by continuous learning and professional growth. His career at Canara Bank spanned 32 years, culminating in his transition to the Wellness domain in 2006.

His methodology revolves around personalised coaching, scientifically validated wellness products, and a holistic approach to health. He believes in the power of hydration, nutrition, and mental motivation to elevate overall well-being. His books, such as "Hydrate to Elevate" and "Quantum Leap to Success," reflect his commitment to sharing knowledge and empowering others to achieve peak performance.

Throughout his career, he has earned numerous qualifications, including a Diploma in Cellular Nutrition Therapy, a Certificate in Emotional Freedom Techniques, and an International Hydration Specialist designation. His work has been recognised globally with awards such as the "Doctor of Honours," "Knights of Charity," and "Knight Commander" from Medicina Alternativa, Colombo.

He is presently associated with his own wellness enterprise "Success Life Creation" since 2009. The primary aim is to establish a "World of Wellness" by providing "Continuous Education Programmes, Mind Motivation, Life-changing Transformational Sessions" on specific themes and areas of research.

He is the mentor of M/S Renatus Wellness Pvt. Ltd, one of the fastest evolving direct sales enterprises dealing with scientifically validated wellness products for the last 5 years. He is a senior global distributor of Enagic India Kangen Water for the last 8 years.

You may explore his website, read the latest blog posts, and discover how his services can transform your life. Whether you seek personal wellness coaching, corporate training, or motivational sessions, you are invited to embark on a journey towards a healthier, more fulfilling life.

Web: https://www.successlifecreation.com